JANSON GOLDSTEIN
WORK

JANSON GOLDSTEIN
WORK

Edited with an Introduction by Andrew Sessa

Published in Australia in 2015 by

The Images Publishing Group Pty Ltd

ABN 89 059 734 431

6 Bastow Place, Mulgrave, Victoria 3170, Australia

Tel: +61 3 9561 5544 Fax: +61 3 9561 4860

books@imagespublishing.com

www.imagespublishing.com

Copyright © The Images Publishing Group Pty Ltd 2015

The Images Publishing Group Reference Number: 1168

All rights reserved. Apart from any fair dealing for the purposes of private study, research, criticism or review as permitted under the Copyright Act, no part of this publication may be reproduced, stored in a retrieval system or transmitted in any form by any means, electronic, mechanical, photocopying, recording or otherwise, without the written permission of the publisher.

National Library of Australia Cataloguing-in-Publication entry

Title:	Janson Goldstein: Work / Mark Janson, Hal Goldstein and Steven Scuro.
ISBN:	9781864706062 (hardback)
Subjects:	Janson Goldstein LLP (Firm)
	Architectural firms—New York (N.Y.)
	Architects—New York (N.Y.)
	Architecture, Modern—21st century.
	Interior decoration.
Dewey Number:	720.97471

Graphic designer: Ryan Marshall

Pre-publishing services by United Graphic Pte Ltd, Singapore

Printed on 150gsm GPrint Smooth paper by Everbest Printing Co. Ltd., in Hong Kong/China

IMAGES has included on its website a page for special notices in relation to this and our other publications. Please visit www.imagespublishing.com.

Contents

7	Introduction

Commercial Work

12	Andaz West Hollywood
26	Armani Casa
30	Calvin Klein Company Store
36	Calvin Klein Underwear
42	Continental Hyatt House
44	Coty Inc. Executive Office Suite
46	db Bistro Moderne
52	Eckō Unltd. Corporate Headquarters and Showrooms
54	Emporio Armani Soho
58	Flatiron Luxury Loft Residences
62	Holt Renfrew Flagships
76	Holt Renfrew Flagship – Next Generation
78	Holt Renfrew Men
86	hr2 Quartier DIX30
90	Intermix
98	Intermix Meatpacking
104	KBOND
106	Kohler / Ann Sacks
112	LVMH Corporate Offices
116	New York Velodrome
120	Ogilvy Montreal
124	Park Avenue Plaza Public Atrium
128	Rocket Dog Brands Corporate Headquarters
136	Saks Fifth Avenue
140	Salvatore Ferragamo
146	The Breakers Palm Beach Retail Shops
150	Times Square Adaptive Reuse
154	Times Square Commercial Development
158	TSE Soho
164	W Hotel Lexington Avenue
168	5 Star Hotel and Residences
174	1200 New Hampshire Avenue NW
180	1345 Avenue of the Americas

Residential Work

186	Bedford Guesthouse
192	Central Park West Residence
198	Cortlandt Manor Residence
200	East Hampton Residence
212	Greenwich Village Loft
220	Hudson Guesthouse
222	London Terrace Penthouse
232	Manhattan Townhouse
240	Mid Century Residence
248	Red Hook Residence
253	Acknowledgements
255	Photography Credits

Introduction
by Andrew Sessa

Upon entering a building by Janson Goldstein—whether a residence, a retail space, a hotel or a public environment—one is immediately struck by several key hallmarks of the architects' approach to design. Graceful open plans allow for multiple appealing avenues of exploration. Abundant natural light filters in from carefully placed glass walls, windows and skylights, intelligently illuminating some elements while casting others into shadow, lending form and shape to the overall structure. Regardless of a project's specific style, a spare elegance prevails, mitigated by a warmth and richness of materials and a disciplined attention to finishes and details. There is a rigor, a clarity of vision and purpose, behind every spatial move, each piece of furniture, every fixture and fitting. Janson Goldstein's buildings telegraph a clear identity, a specific sense of place. Giving equal attention to intimate domestic spaces and grand public projects, the firm makes architecture that connects to, and embraces, both the individual and the community at large.

Take, for example, a 900-square-meter, six-bedroom vacation home in East Hampton, the storied hamlet on the East End of New York's Long Island. Seeking to subtly set the structure within the historic character of the village setting, but wanting to combine the traditional with the contemporary, Janson Goldstein developed an aesthetic language for the house that's evocative of the Shaker style. The architects channeled Shaker's strong but simple geometries to create a low gabled roof and gray-shingled façade whose six-over-six windows march across it in a grid. A great room fills one ground-level wing, its bleached-oak flooring and exposed posts and beams visually uniting its various spaces for cooking, dining and relaxing. Large windows and glass doors let in air and natural light, as does a 13-meter-long skylight running the length of the gabled ceiling. Upstairs, the bedrooms sit off one side of a single long hallway, further maximizing the movement of light and air. Outside and in, the home translates an intimate understanding of its place and its purpose into clean, clear, elegant lines, and spaces that are at once both classic and modern.

From the very first days of Janson Goldstein's founding, in 1995, the partners of the New York–based firm have based their practice on a pair of guiding principles: the seamless integration of architecture and interior design, and the cultivation and curation of a portfolio that would evidence a broad diversity of scale, program and building typology.

In the two decades since then, the firm's three partners—Hal Goldstein, Mark Janson and Steven Scuro—have stayed true to these tenets, working simultaneously from the outside in and the inside out to make spaces that have ranged in size and scope, style and type from a stripped-down 120-square-meter guesthouse in Upstate New York to a sparkling, 12,000-square-meter luxury department store in downtown Vancouver; from a double-height, glass-enclosed entry pavilion for an office building in Washington, D.C., to a 240-room hotel and restaurant in West Hollywood.

Despite this variety, the partners' specific point of view and their unique process have remained consistent, guided first and foremost by those primary principles. That point of view, it should be noted, is not an aesthetic one—beholden to a particular style or school—but is instead philosophic. They believe in rigorous, purposeful place-making born out of a project's specific and unique context: its siting, its circumstance, and its client's needs.

Their process, as a result, proves equal parts inquisitive, inclusive and collaborative. Students of human behavior, the architects use meetings with clients to determine how people experience a place, how they interact with space and how they feel about those places and spaces. They thrive on dialogue, making it their job to listen and interpret, probe and reinforce.

Out of this process, they develop an identity for each building. They consider proportion paramount, creating plans and elevations that telegraph purity and restraint. To give life to these spaces, they rely on the power of natural light, opening buildings to their surroundings and to the sky with glass used in myriad innovative ways. Indeed, they often partner with manufacturers to develop new materials that take advantage of contemporary technology. In Vancouver, for example, the architects worked with the city's Nathan Allan Glass Studios to create the unique, quilted-looking 'pillowed' glass that clads the façade of luxury retailer Holt Renfrew's flagship; and at Midtown Manhattan's Park Avenue Plaza, they collaborated with Germany's Schott AG to design the illuminated glass tubes that line the lobby walls.

Although the firm has worked for some of the world's most famous fashion, retail and hospitality brands—Giorgio Armani, Salvatore Ferragamo, Calvin Klein and LVMH; Holt Renfrew and Saks Fifth Avenue; Hyatt and Starwood— the architects' practice is not swayed by changes in style or trend. Nor have they limited themselves to a single historic vernacular or aesthetic idiom. Rather, their designs strive for timelessness.

If Janson Goldstein's buildings do owe a debt to modernism, it is born less out of deference or homage to the 20th-century masters they admire (Mies van der Rohe, Eero Saarinen and Louis Kahn, among others) and more out of a commitment to the values these modern icons established—a dedication to open, flowing space; ample natural light; honesty of structure; refinement of proportion; and the seamless integration of architecture and interior design.

The firm's brand of modernism has a warmth and a richness achieved by an often complex layering of materials and textures, and by frequent thoughtful collaborations with the individual craftsman and artisans who create custom pieces for their spaces. This has often become most apparent in the firm's interiors for its residential commissions, like that of a 240-square-meter penthouse in London Terrace, a square-block-sized prewar apartment complex in New York City's Chelsea neighborhood. Completed for a prominent pair of fashion executives and eventually featured on the cover of *Architectural Digest*, Janson Goldstein's design for the apartment reinvented a dark, warren-like four-bedroom as a light and lofty one-bedroom, with a series of 22 new French doors, and casement windows opening up to a wraparound terrace and 180-degree city views.

For the interiors, which evoke the spirit of the building's 1920s origins, the firm collaborated closely with the clients, designing the spaces around pieces already in the owners' collections of furniture and art, as well as those acquired specifically for the new home. In the living room, a graphic carpet forms a base for furnishings found at flea markets and antiques shops around the world, which the architects augmented with a dark marble mantelpiece and lacquered millwork and bookshelves, all of their own design. They also re-covered vintage upholstered pieces—a Knoll bench here, a Jens Risom armchair and ottoman there—in textured, tailored textiles such as grey flannel and tuxedo velvet. The finished spaces are both old and new, classic and contemporary, cool but welcoming.

Site-specific design solutions, warm layers of luxurious materials and artisanal collaborations characterize the firm's copious retail work, too. A boutique in Manhattan's Meatpacking District for the multi-venue, high-fashion brand Intermix—for whom the firm has created more than 40 stores—integrates pieces of the historic High Line elevated railroad into part of its ceiling structure. Elsewhere in the shop, light floods in from floor-to-ceiling street-side windows, and fumed-oak planks curve down from the ceiling to cover the walls and become the floor in the fitting area, creating a cozy wooden cocoon that envelops customers. The architects commissioned New York–based designer Bec Brittain to create a constellation of custom bronze pendant lamps, whose light plays off the 1,600 curved aluminum panels of a 3-meter-tall ribbon-like hanging screen, activating the space above shoppers' heads. This evocative environment feels as filled with personal, local touches as the London Terrace penthouse, designed to realize the brand's ambitions and the customers' dreams, just as that residence did for its owners.

As they move forward into their next 20 years, the partners of Janson Goldstein continue to seek new answers to old questions—How do we use and occupy space? What is the experience and the emotion a place should convey? As ever, they find solutions in their rigorous, thoughtful design process; their commitment to client collaboration; and their firmly held belief that the most successful architecture and interior design is born out of thoughtful consideration of, and care for, each commission's specific context, circumstances and aspirations.

COMMERCIAL WORK

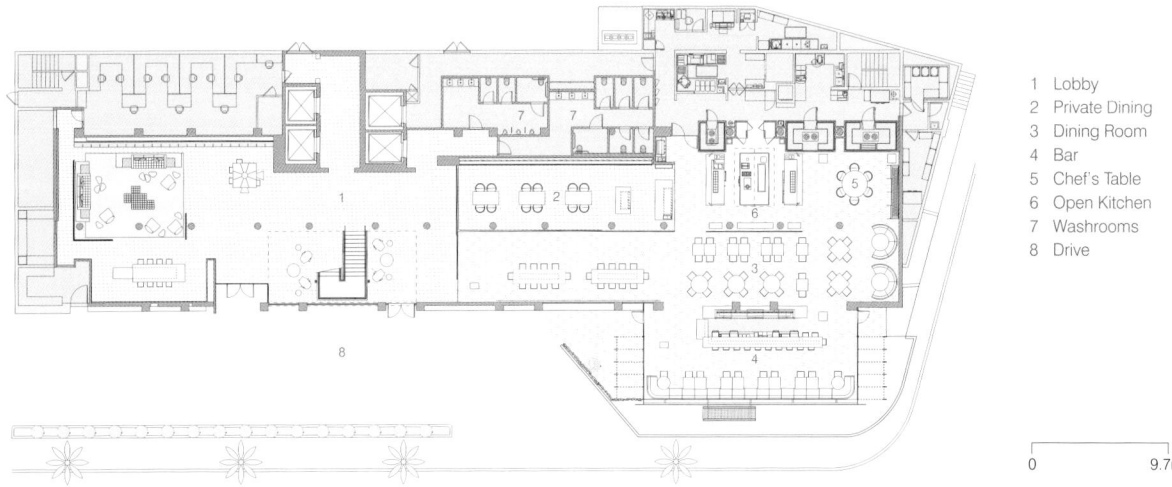

Ground Floor Plan

1 Lobby
2 Private Dining
3 Dining Room
4 Bar
5 Chef's Table
6 Open Kitchen
7 Washrooms
8 Drive

Andaz West Hollywood

West Hollywood, CA
2009

Begun in 2004 as a renovation of Los Angeles's Continental Hyatt House (once a Sunset Strip hangout for rock-and-roll royalty), this project became the American debut of Hyatt's Andaz concept, and an entirely new scheme—conceived as an icon for an emerging brand—replaced the original notion. Inspired by the mid-century aesthetic of the 1960s property, the ultimate design pays homage to such masterful L.A. modernists as Richard Neutra and Pierre Koenig. It encloses the balconies of the west-facing rooms in glass to reinvent the building's Sunset Boulevard façade, expanding those rooms into mini-suites with impressive views. A new steel-and-glass pavilion at the base of the hotel's tower, with a site-specific installation by artist Jacob Hashimoto, houses the hotel's restaurant and simultaneously serves as a new marker for the property on Sunset.

Andaz West Hollywood 17

Andaz West Hollywood

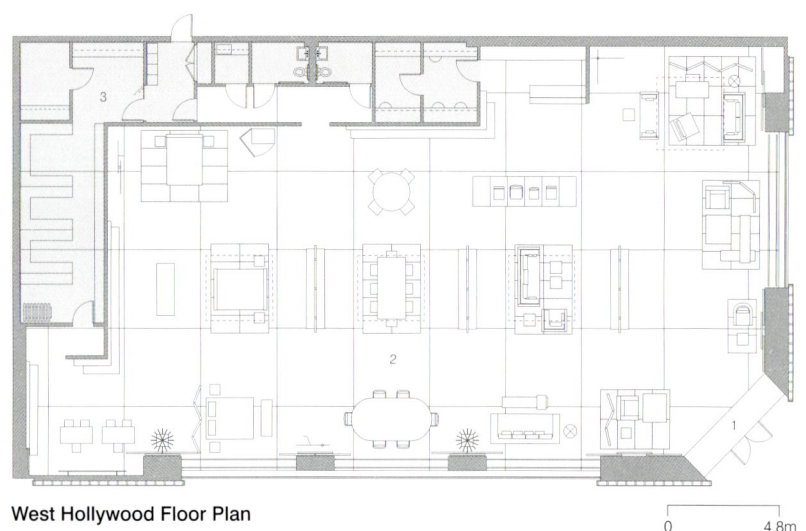

1 Entry
2 Retail
3 Receiving Area

West Hollywood Floor Plan

0   4.8m

Armani Casa

West Hollywood, CA
2001
New York, NY
2001

These stores introduced Giorgio Armani's new Armani Casa home collection to the U.S. market. For the inaugural location, in New York's Soho district, Mr. Armani found inspiration in the neighborhood's distinctive lofts. Their aesthetic and atmosphere translated into a design characterized by open spaces, concrete floors and strong, sculptural shapes—a concept continued at the second shop, in West Hollywood. Both locations use large, prominent skylights to illuminate and give form to spare white-on-white spaces. In New York, a dramatic glass-and-stone staircase sits beneath an angled skylight filling the full width of the store, while in West Hollywood, low walls divide a single level into distinct areas for different product categories, with each zone lit from above by a pyramid-shaped skylight.

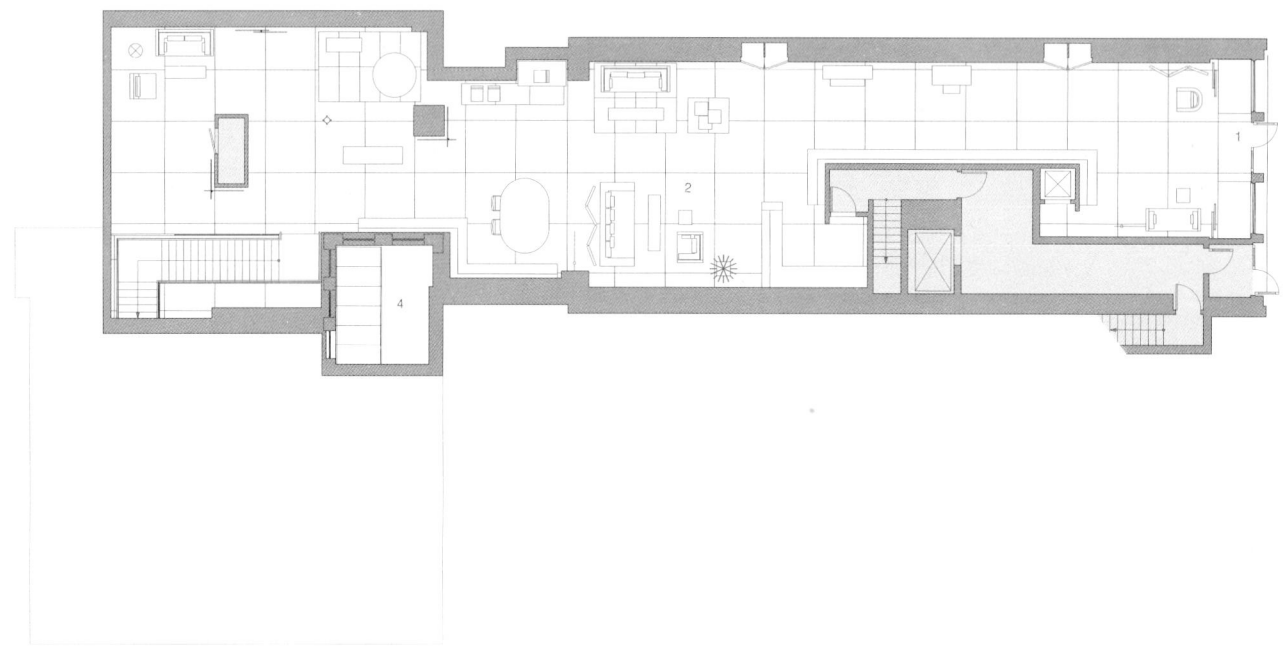

Soho Ground Floor Plan

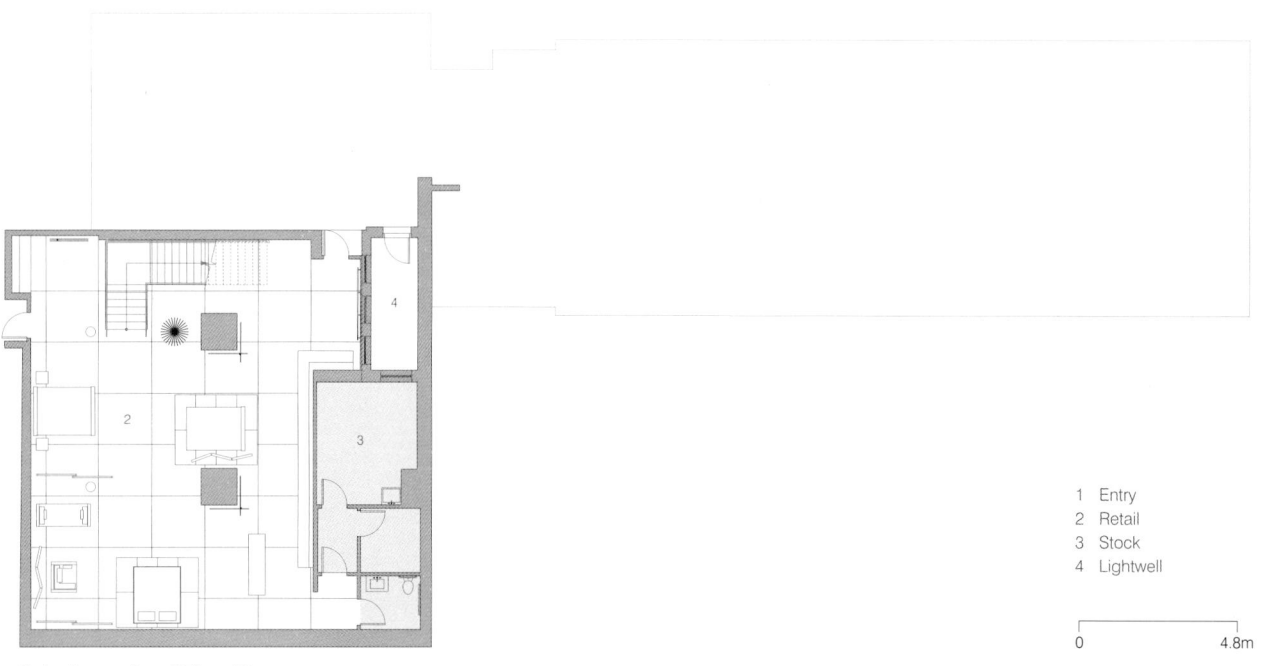

Soho Lower Level Floor Plan

1 Entry
2 Retail
3 Stock
4 Lightwell

0   4.8m

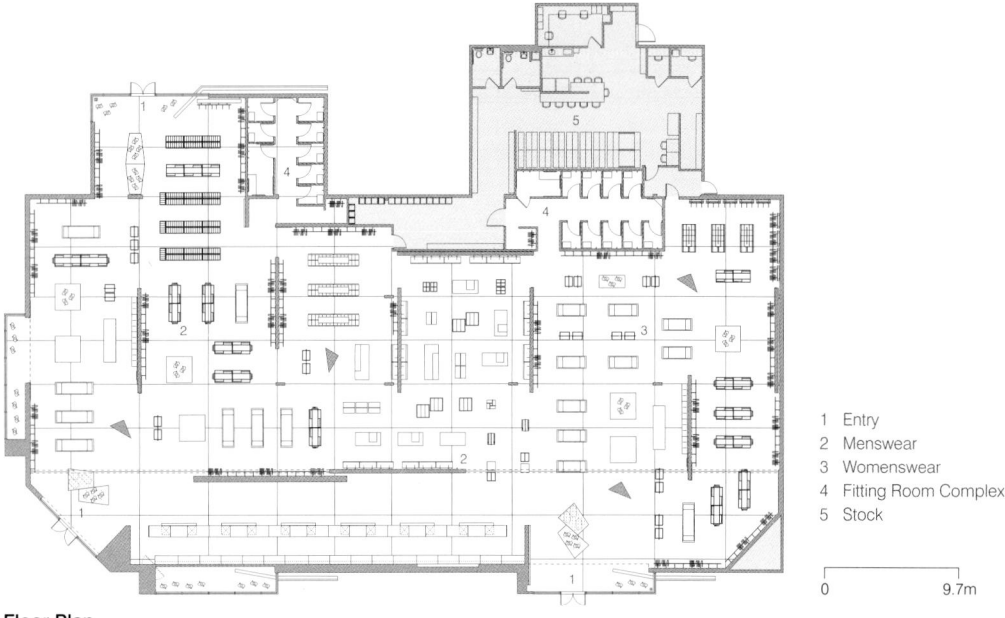

1 Entry
2 Menswear
3 Womenswear
4 Fitting Room Complex
5 Stock

0   9.7m

Floor Plan

Calvin Klein Company Store

Las Vegas, NV
2013
Harriman, NY
2012

Sunrise, FL
2012
Vaughan, ON
2012

Each approximately 1860 square meters in size and designed as high-volume, high-energy environments, these company stores represent Calvin Klein products in the highly competitive off-price market. The spaces combine men's and women's clothing, previously sold in separate storefronts, as well as footwear and accessories. The new stores make ample use of Calvin Klein's graphic and advertising materials as iconic brand touchstones, their schemes incorporating open ceilings and concrete floors, as well as exposed HVAC and lighting systems. These elements both address the budget considerations inherent in this typology and become emblems of a loft-like, sophisticated atmosphere that appeals to the younger demographic these stores target and serve.

Calvin Klein Company Store

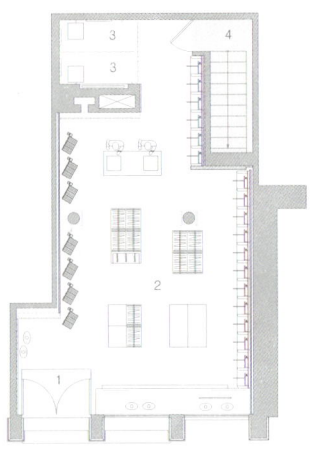

Soho Floor Plan

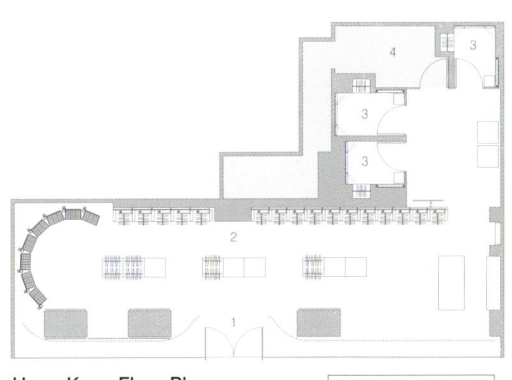

Hong Kong Floor Plan

1 Entry
2 Retail
3 Fitting Room
4 Stock

0   4.8m

Calvin Klein Underwear

Hong Kong
2014
New York, NY
2011
London, UK
2008

This new store model for Calvin Klein Underwear represents a departure from the brand's previously minimalist aesthetic. In this concept, executed worldwide, custom-created sculptural forms house all products, with each form responding to a specific item's packaging and display requirements, as well as its unique features—a sheer intimate, for example, is backlit to highlight its fabric and color. To reduce construction time and cost, the stores consist predominantly of prefabricated elements, with on-site work largely limited to the creation of a neutral background. Otherwise, the sculptural forms containing the merchandise define the design of each space, putting paramount emphasis on the product and resulting in a dynamic environment, even within relatively small confines.

Calvin Klein Underwear

Calvin Klein Underwear

Continental Hyatt House

West Hollywood, CA
2004

Reimagining Los Angeles's Continental Hyatt House—a Sunset Strip home away from home for many oft-misbehaving rock legends—this scheme seeks to recapture some of the property's bad-boy rock-and-roll heritage, letting it live up to its reputation as 'the Riot House.' The design takes as its inspiration a film-noir reinterpretation of the property's 1960s modernist vibe, with a new façade, new public spaces and a new rooftop terrace and swimming pool offering long views of the L.A. basin to the west and the Hollywood Hills to the east. Before beginning this renovation, Hyatt decided to turn the hotel into the first American outpost of its new Andaz brand, and a new iconic concept was developed for that debut. (See page 12.)

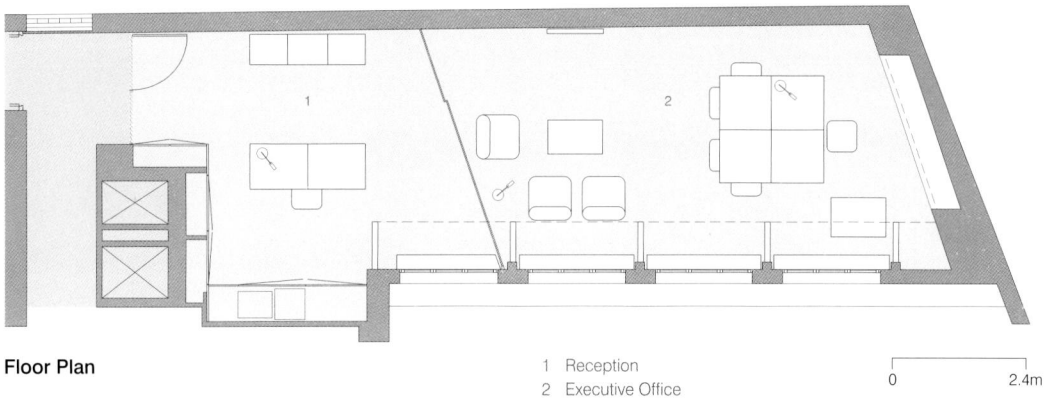

Floor Plan

1 Reception
2 Executive Office

0 — 2.4m

Coty Inc. Executive Office Suite

Paris, France
2001

This Parisian office suite, created for the chief executive of the French beauty and fragrance company Coty Inc., is a study in minimalism, taking the inspiration for its spare design from the crystal glass of the company's fragrance bottles. The sole components of the office are an executive desk-cum-conference table and a small seating area. Brilliant-white Venetian plaster covers the walls, while white high-tech automotive paint finishes the steel furniture. All the glass used—from the conference table to the walls—is crystal clear and low iron.

Coty Inc. Executive Office Suite

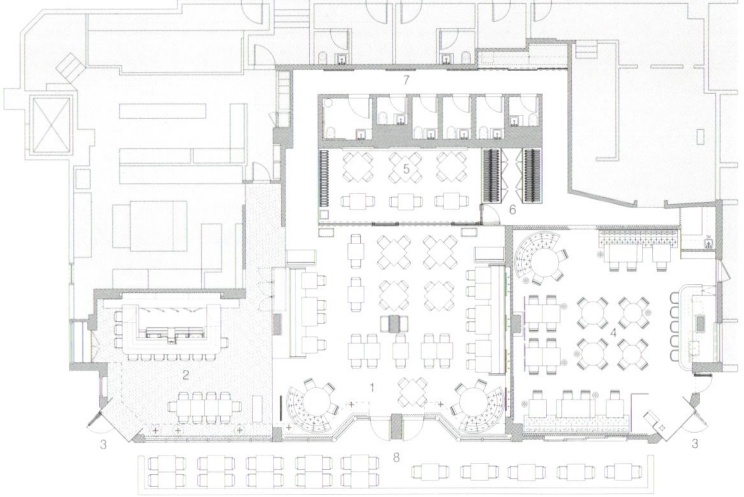

Floor Plan

1 db Bistro Moderne Dining
2 Bar
3 Entry
4 Lumière Dining
5 Private Dining
6 Wine Cellar
7 Washrooms
8 Sidewalk Cafe

0   4.8m

db Bistro Moderne

Vancouver, BC
2008

Created for Michelin-starred chef Daniel Boulud, this project includes the white-tablecloth French restaurant Lumière and more casual db Bistro Moderne. The latter particularly exhibits a deft touch with materials, tones and textures, its inviting atmosphere putting a unique modern spin on the classic Parisian bistro. The bar area features herringbone travertine flooring, a zinc bar top and, behind the bar, woven, polished stainless-steel surfaces framed in red eel skin. Custom handcrafted glass pendants, based on a 1960s Italian design, illuminate the space. Beyond a screen of saw-tooth-textured bronze glass, rolled-steel channeled fixtures illuminate the dining room, where custom-designed chairs of distressed oak and oxblood leather complement banquets in brown- and copper-colored woven leather. A private dining and wine room presents wine racks made of oil-quenched steel and a wall covered in rich red and brown leather tiles.

db Bistro Moderne 49

db Bistro Moderne

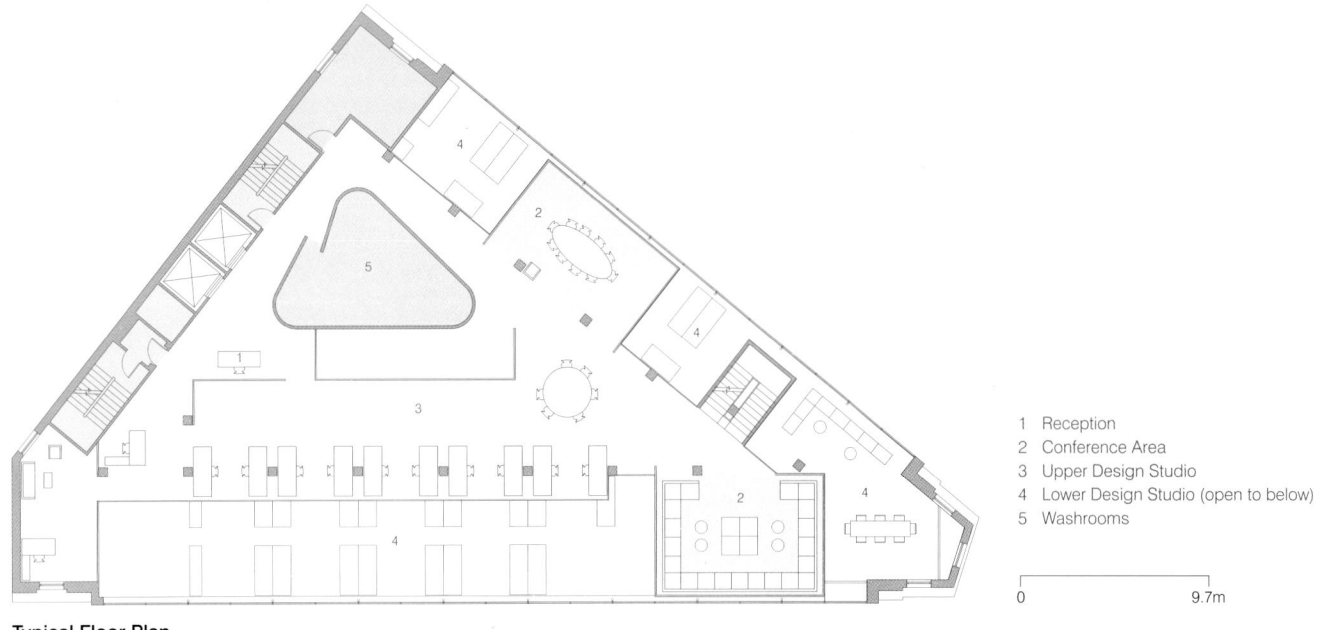

Typical Floor Plan

1 Reception
2 Conference Area
3 Upper Design Studio
4 Lower Design Studio (open to below)
5 Washrooms

Eckō Unltd. Corporate Headquarters and Showrooms

Perth Amboy, NJ
2004

Eckō Unltd. commissioned the conversion of a 12-story, Depression-era landmark in Perth Amboy, NJ, into new headquarters. A retail space occupies the base, with offices, showrooms and design studios above, plus a new penthouse with gym, locker rooms and a half-size basketball court. Tasked by the urban fashion brand to develop shared, hierarchy-free workspaces, but required by the existing structure to divide these spaces across three floors, the new scheme suggests a unique solution: it removes perimeter floor plates and clads upper levels in glass to create a shared, three-level environment around the building's edges. Cantilevered glass boxes within this atrium house showrooms and meeting spaces, while a glass-enclosed stair tower connects to the penthouse, itself clad in polished stainless steel to reflect, and blur with, the sky.

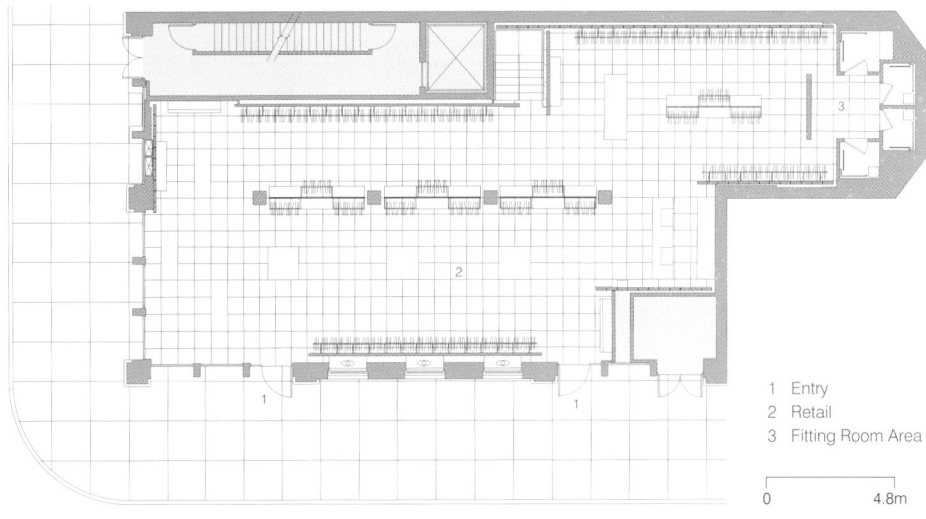

Floor Plan

1 Entry
2 Retail
3 Fitting Room Area

0   4.8m

Emporio Armani Soho

New York, NY
2002

In contrast to the series of Emporio Armani stores throughout the U.S. designed in a single common idiom, this location stands as a one-of-a-kind environment. Although the space is modest in size, the brand saw it as a flagship, stocking a spare, curated assortment. Mr. Armani's concept for the store, which sits on a prominent corner in New York's Soho, sought to represent the unique vibe of its downtown location and customer base. To that end, high and low, old and new, rough and refined sit in poignant juxtaposition here: a honed-granite floor abuts sandblasted concrete-block walls, for example, against which sit the store's sophisticated offerings. At the center of the space, frosted acrylic, lit from within, surrounds original cast-iron columns—a ghost of the past seen through a modern shroud.

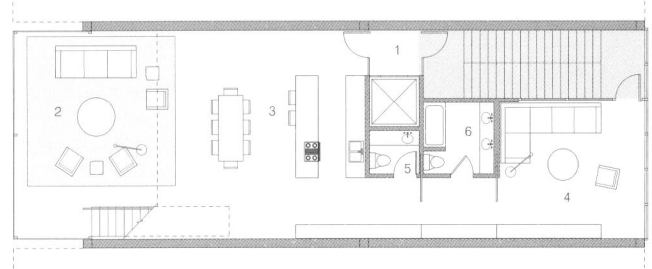

Typical Duplex Floor Plan

1 Elevator Lobby
2 Living Room
3 Kitchen / Dining Area
4 Media / Library
5 Powder Room
6 Bathroom

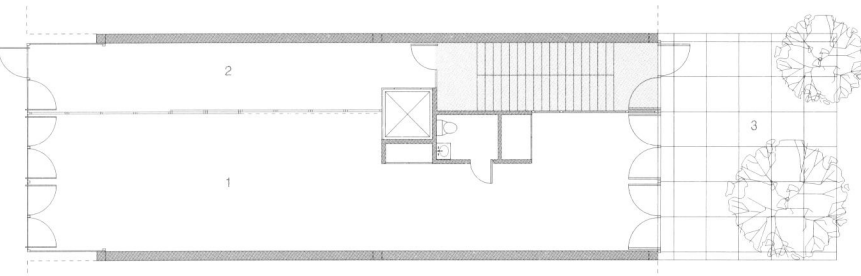

Ground Floor Plan

1 Retail Tenent
2 Condominium Entrance
3 Garden

0   4.8m

Flatiron Luxury Loft Residences

New York, NY
1999

This mixed-use, luxury residential and retail project, which rises mid-block between Sixth and Seventh Avenues in New York's Flatiron District, evokes the warmth and clean lines of Isamu Noguchi's 1950s Akari light sculptures. It juxtaposes a two-story retail base and duplex condominium apartments above, both sheathed in bronze-toned glass, with one-level condo units that each have a terrace and a recessed clear-glass wall. By alternating the double-height apartments with those of a single story, a series of lantern-like illuminated stacked cubes emerges. Inside, the loft-like apartments' clean, open plans allow for easy flow from front to back, with a large, double-height space in each duplex facing the street. Residents share a ground-level garden and a rooftop terrace.

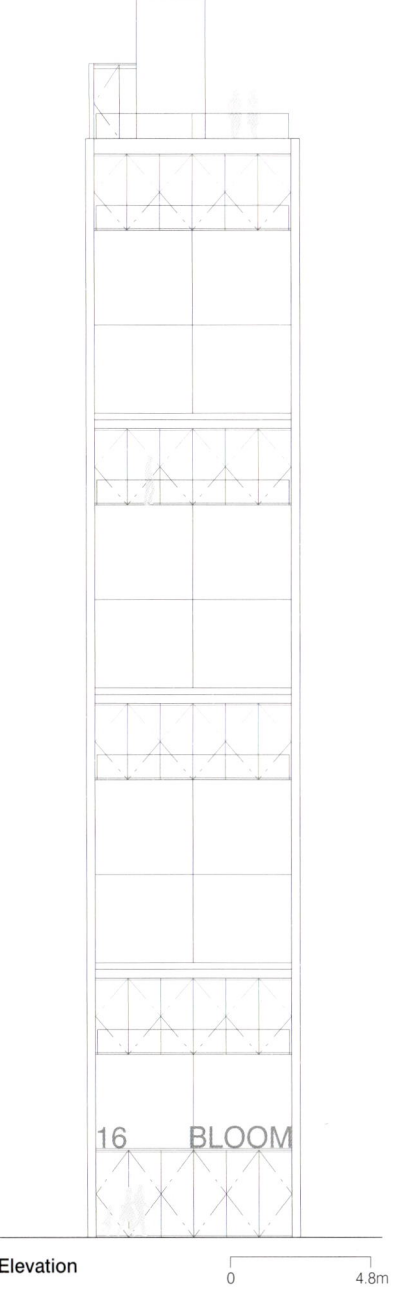

Elevation 0 4.8m

Flatiron Luxury Loft Residences 59

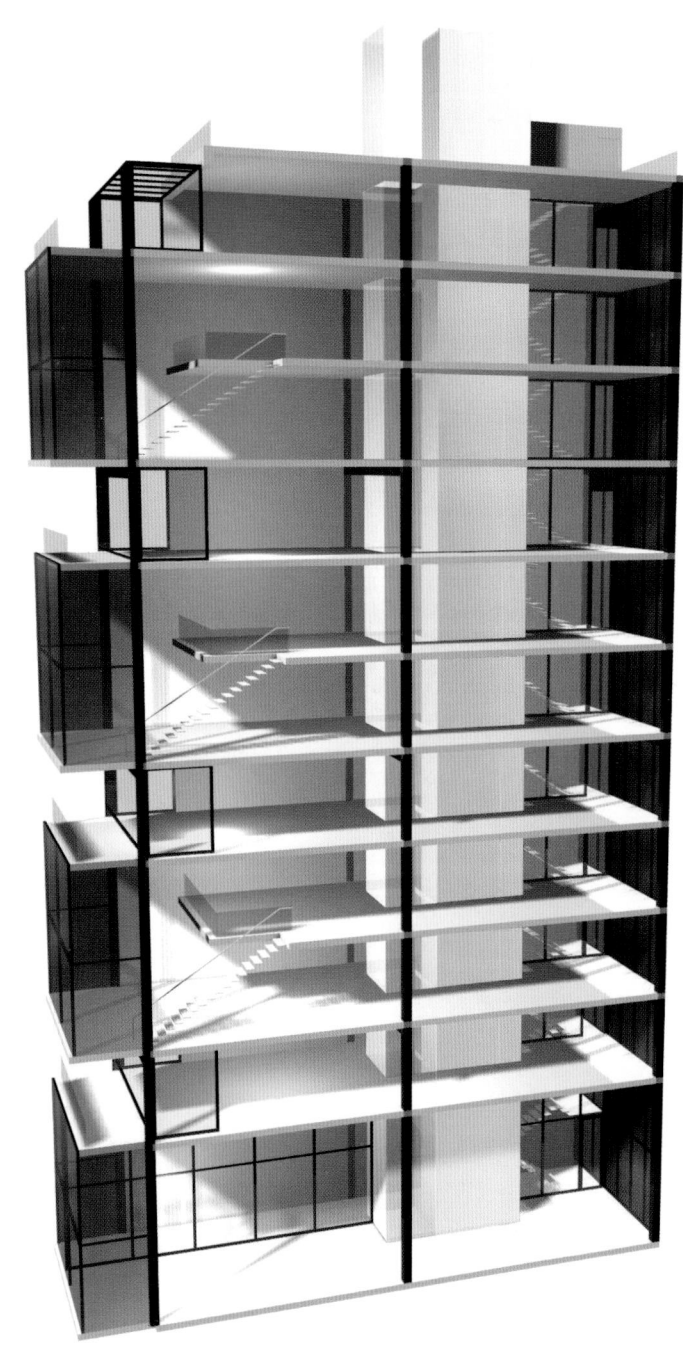

Vancouver Site Plan 1 Holt Renfrew 2 Pacific Center 0 — 61m

Holt Renfrew Flagships

Toronto, ON
2013
Calgary, AB
2009
Vancouver, BC
2007

The continuation of a long-term partnership dating to 2005, these new concepts for Canadian luxury retailer Holt Renfrew's three flagships share design DNA but are adapted to their unique settings. The first, in Vancouver, breaks long-established department-store tropes, abandoning the lifeless, windowless brick box with interiors defined by 'hard' aisles (stone) and 'soft' pads (carpet). Instead, high-tech glass clads the exterior, and luminous white-marble floors unify light-filled interiors. Created with Vancouver's Nathan Allan Glass Studios, the iconic 'pillowed' glass panels have a quilted appearance, their convex cells refracting light differently throughout the day. At the building's heart, a three-story atrium sits beneath a giant skylight as a dynamic public attraction, connecting the 12,000-square-meter space's shopping levels. The Calgary flagship adapts this successful formula, anchoring downtown's Core development.

Holt Renfrew Flagships

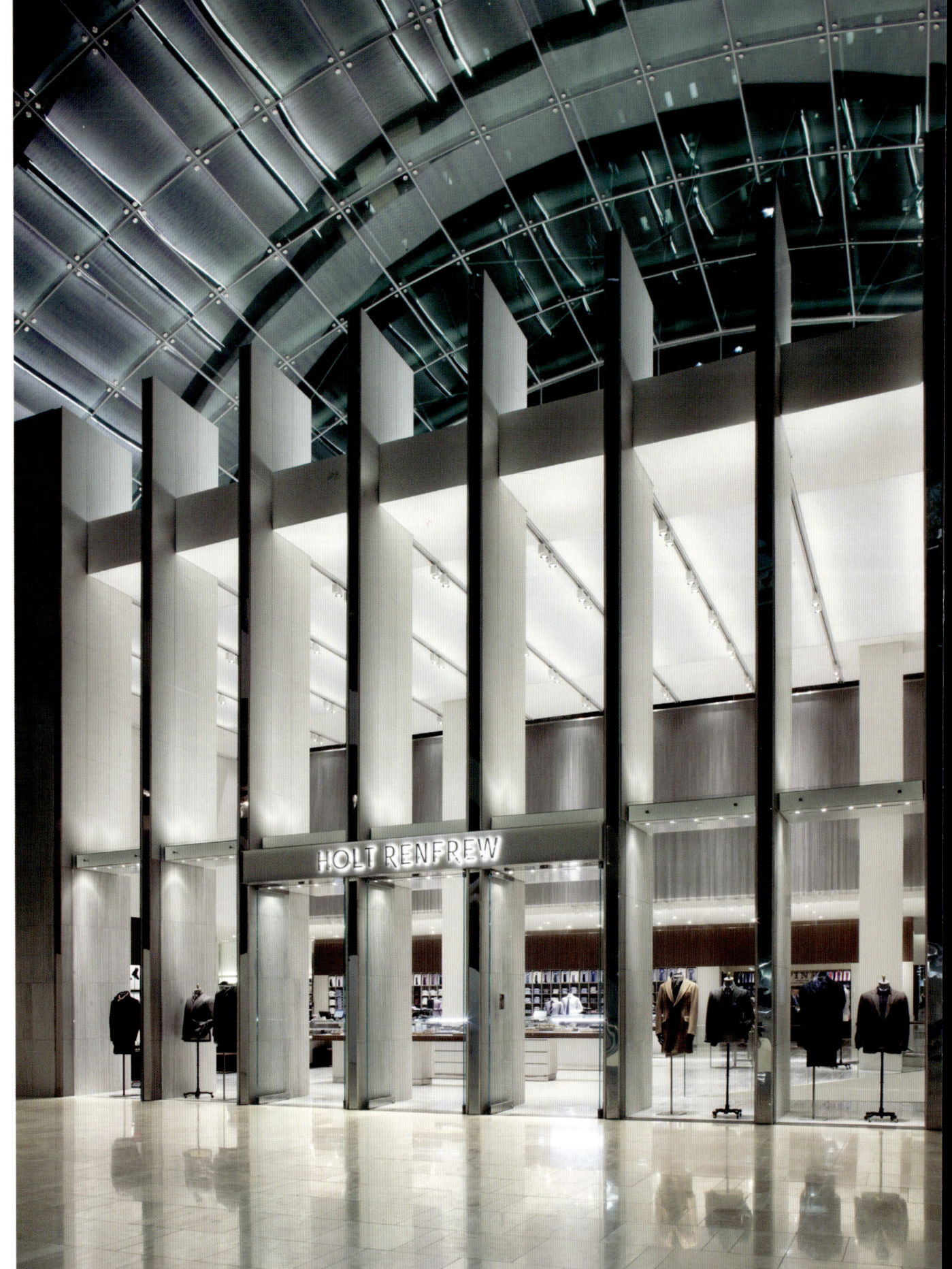

Holt Renfrew Flagships

Holt Renfrew Flagship – Next Generation

Mississauga, ON
2016

This freestanding 11,150-square-meter store in the West Toronto suburb of Mississauga represents the next generation in large-scale luxury retailing for the high-end Canadian department store Holt Renfrew. Sheathed entirely in an iconic and proprietary glass façade created exclusively for Holt Renfrew by Janson Goldstein, the structure represents a key element of downtown Mississauga's new master plan. The building stands as a glowing glass box whose scale and prominence equal the area's other major landmarks, including a performing arts center and city hall, which sit directly opposite. The flagship sets a new standard for department-store design, employing natural daylight to illuminate the interiors of its entire perimeter, and allowing visual communication between indoors and out.

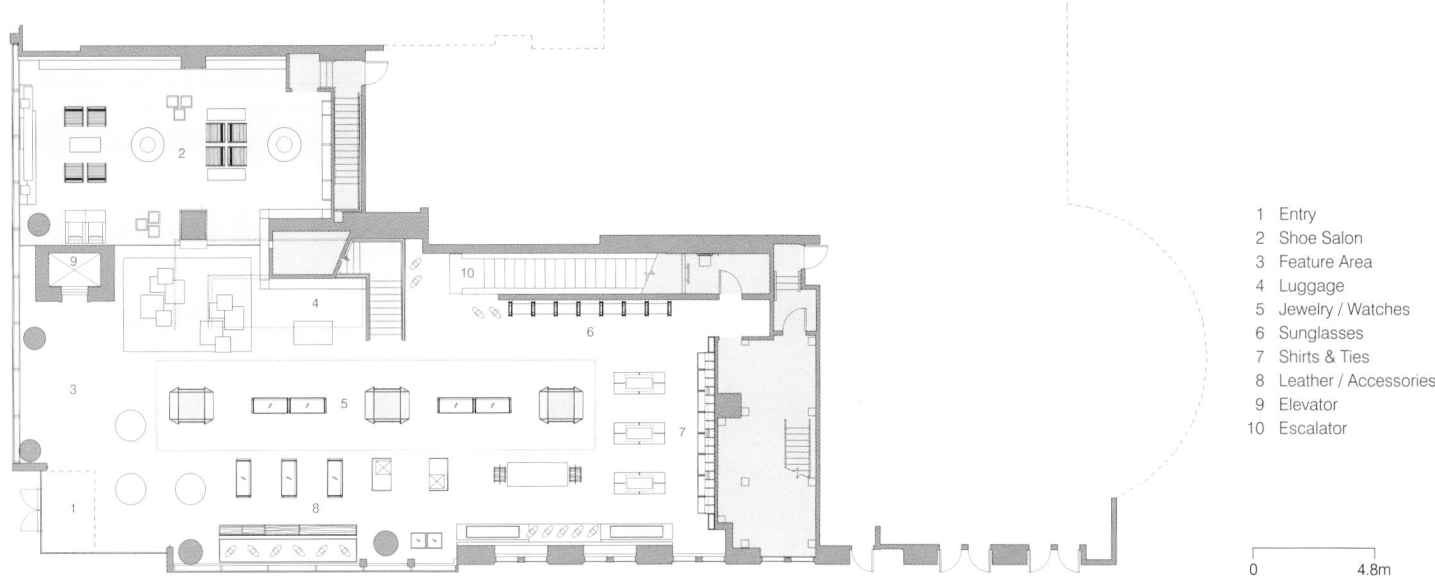

Ground Floor Plan

1 Entry
2 Shoe Salon
3 Feature Area
4 Luggage
5 Jewelry / Watches
6 Sunglasses
7 Shirts & Ties
8 Leather / Accessories
9 Elevator
10 Escalator

Holt Renfrew Men

Toronto, ON
2014

Holt Renfrew's debut stand-alone men's concept store, this 1500-square-meter space on Toronto's fashionable Bloor Street represents a departure for the Canadian luxury retailer, its masculine design resembling a private club as much as a store. On the main level, internally lit shelving in gray-stained white oak and blackened stainless steel surrounds central columns. A custom mosaic-tile floor connects leather goods, jewelry and men's furnishings, while a hand-knotted custom carpet and deep-blue, leather-upholstered, polished-stainless-steel chairs define the footwear area. On the fashion-focused second level—which includes a personal-shopping suite and bespoke-tailoring shop—walnut shutters and herringbone flooring create a residential feel, and a patterned-wool runner marks a circulation path. A double-height structural screen extends through the escalator atrium, creating a strong visual connection between the two floors and providing additional visual-merchandising space.

Second Floor Plan

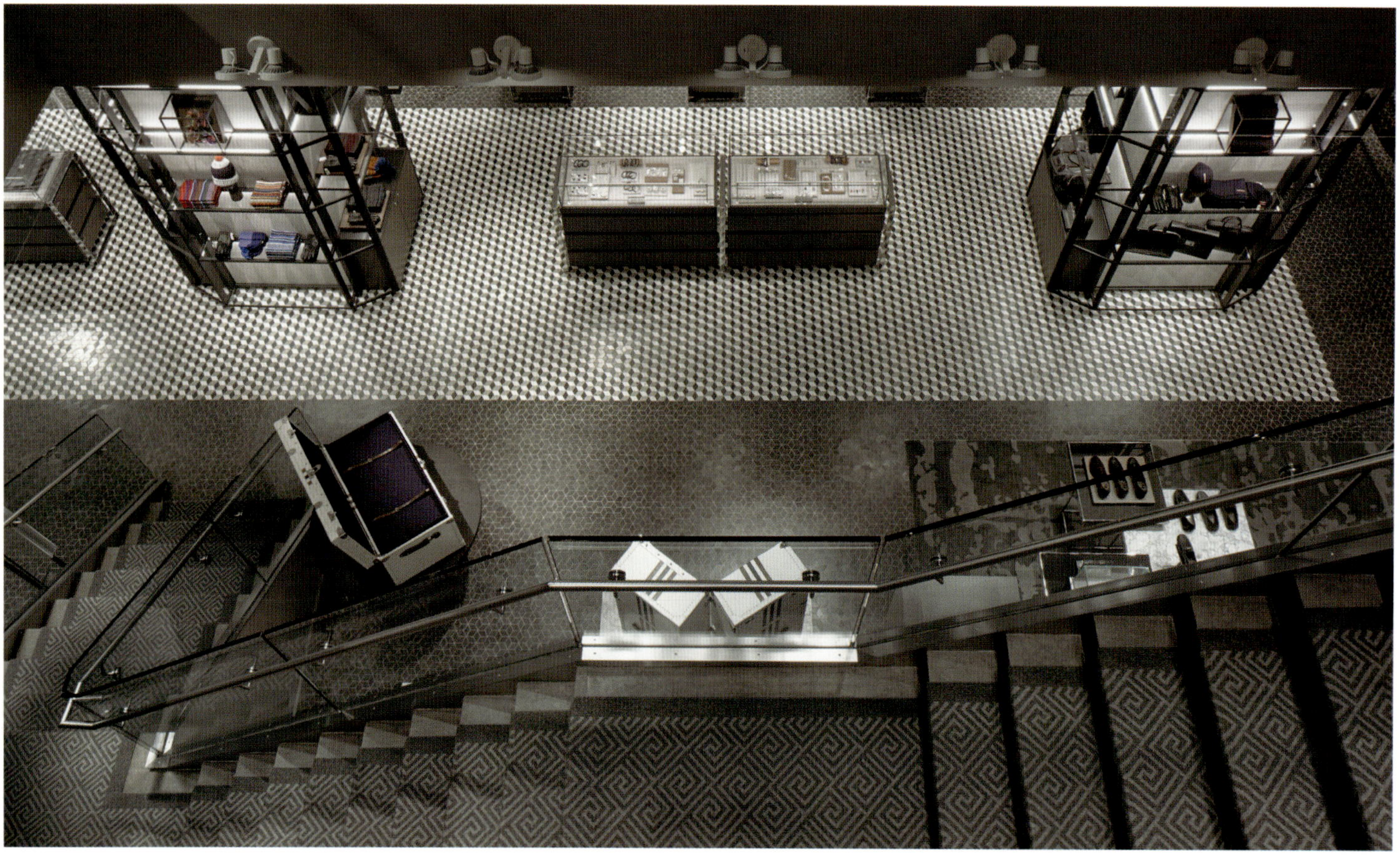

1 Escalator
2 Elevator
3 Fitting Area
4 Personal Shopping Suite
5 Bespoke Tailor Shop
6 Fragrance / Skincare
7 Sartorial
8 Sportswear
9 Outerwear

0   4.8m

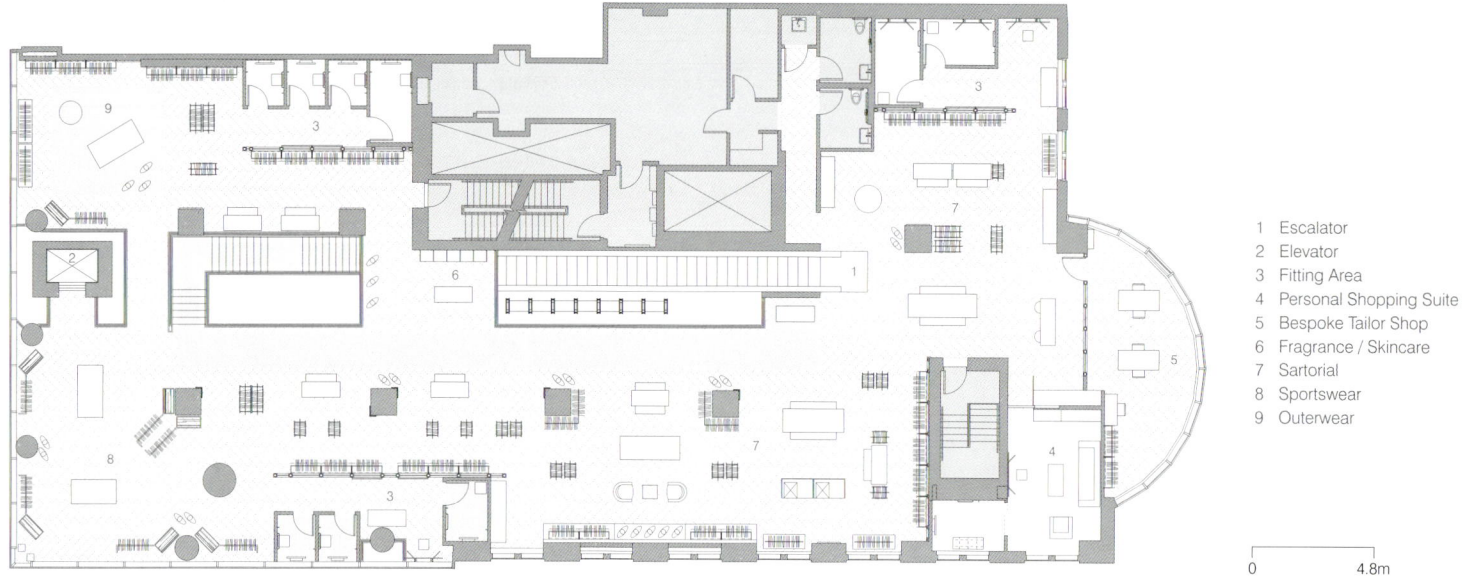

Holt Renfrew Men 85

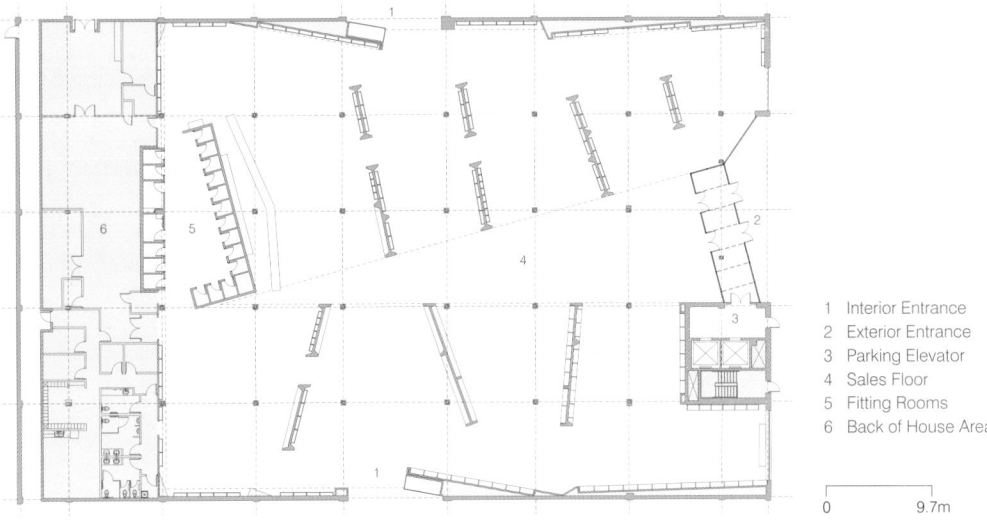

Floor Plan

1 Interior Entrance
2 Exterior Entrance
3 Parking Elevator
4 Sales Floor
5 Fitting Rooms
6 Back of House Area

hr2 Quartier DIX30

Montreal, QC
2013

Designed to introduce Canadian luxury retailer Holt Renfrew's off-price concept, this store stands as a bold brand statement. It occupies the terminus of the central axis of Montreal's Quartier DIX30 development, the facets of its perforated aluminum façade creating a striking sculpture that both captures and reflects daylight and evening illumination. At night, it also glows warmly from within, becoming a canvas for a computerized LED display. The interior proceeds from the forms of the exterior, split into men's and women's halves by a central spine connecting the façade to the cash/wrap opposite. In between, customers browse a series of 'hedges'—3-meter-high walls that both house merchandise and separate different product categories, just as boxwoods divide a garden—then return down the spine to exit through the iconic, light-filtering façade.

hr2 Quartier DIX30

Intermix

Madison Avenue, New York, NY
2014
Soho, New York, NY
2013

Brooklyn, New York, NY
2013
Bowery, New York, NY
2013

Since 2010, Janson Goldstein's collaboration with Intermix has resulted in 40-plus boutiques for the multi-vendor, high-end fashion retailer. A brand-wide visual language unites them, but each store's neighborhood context provides distinct inspiration. For example, on New York's Bowery, a former deli combines elements of the area's bygone punk-rock days (wire-brushed brick, iron-beam racks) with sophisticated furnishings referencing its current fashionable status. In a once industrial and now family-friendly stretch of Brooklyn's Carroll Gardens, a rebuilt brick storefront and largely original interiors embrace the street with a new oversized display window and entry. On Madison Avenue, screens made of darkened bronze, blackened steel, woven bronze and stainless steel reference the Upper East Side's reputation for luxury, while Soho evokes an iconic downtown artist's loft, incorporating cast-iron columns and sculptural elements.

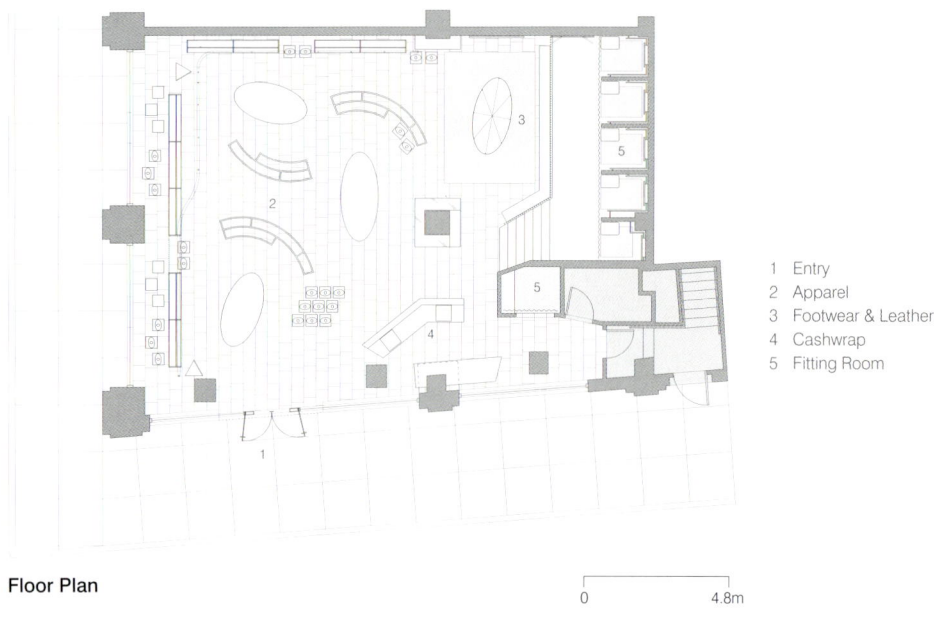

Floor Plan

1 Entry
2 Apparel
3 Footwear & Leather
4 Cashwrap
5 Fitting Room

0　4.8m

Intermix Meatpacking

New York, NY
2011

The first of a new generation of stores designed for the multi-vendor, high-fashion retailer Intermix, this 230-square-meter boutique in Manhattan's Meatpacking district nestles beneath the High Line, the park on the West Side's 1930s-era elevated railroad. In the soaring space, a 3-meter-tall, ribbon-like screen made of 1600 panes of curved, mirror-polished aluminum hangs from the steel track, diffusing and reflecting daylight from floor-to-ceiling windows and site-specific light installations by Brooklyn designer Bec Brittain. In the fitting area, fumed European white oak wraps the floor, walls and ceiling, creating a wooden grotto. Elsewhere, an oversized custom-designed oval ottoman covered in soft, pale-purple leather serves as a central seating element in the footwear area, and antiqued, slightly rusticated black Belgian limestone covers the floor in a random pattern, referencing the neighborhood's cobblestone streets.

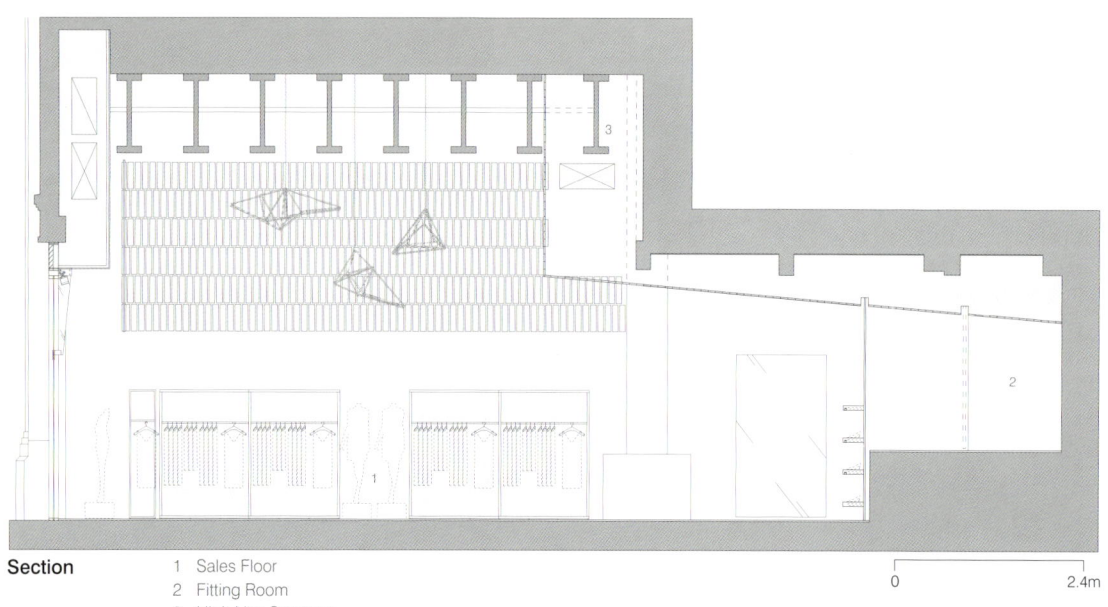

Section
1 Sales Floor
2 Fitting Room
3 High Line Structure

0 2.4m

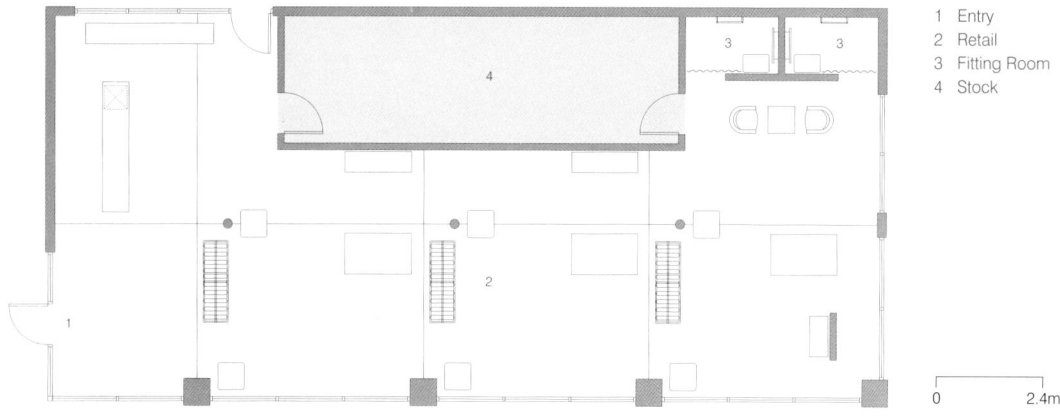

Floor Plan

1 Entry
2 Retail
3 Fitting Room
4 Stock

KBOND

Los Angeles, CA
1999

Owned by, and designed in collaboration with, installation artist Karen Kimmel and her husband, James Bond, this innovative Los Angeles menswear boutique occupied a glass-fronted raw space clearly visible to pedestrians and cars on Beverly Boulevard, especially at night, when it was illuminated from within. Mindful of the brand's desire to integrate artistic interventions, and working with a limited budget, the scheme for the store took creative advantage of existing conditions. Bold but simple sculptural constructions made of theater scrim and gelled fluorescent lighting both divided the space and displayed hanging products, while glass-topped architectural flat files housed folded pieces. Opposite the glazed façade, a 9-meter-long wall became not only a backdrop for the merchandise, but also a blank canvas that a different artist-collaborator would refresh with a new installation every 60 days.

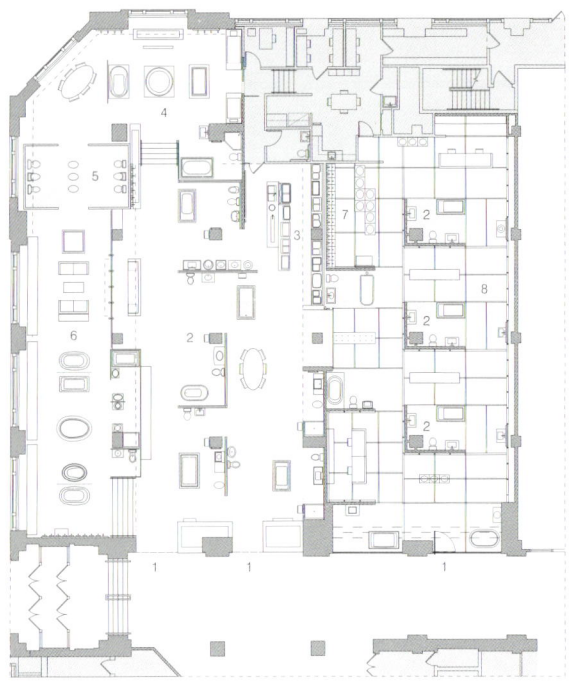

Floor Plan

1 Entry
2 Bath Vignettes
3 Kitchen
4 Whirlpool / Shower
5 Toilets
6 Bath
7 Kallista
8 Tile Library

0   4.8m

Kohler / Ann Sacks

Chicago, IL
2006

Occupying adjacent spaces in Chicago's famed Merchandise Mart, these interrelated projects represent Kohler's first-ever direct-to-consumer retail space, and a new showroom type for Ann Sacks. To maximize its ability to communicate directly with customers, the Kohler space takes the form of a design exhibition devoted to the company's kitchen and bath fixtures, with a clear circular path leading through the individualized galleries created for each product line. As such, it serves multiple functions: brand bastion, retail outlet, product showroom. The design for Ann Sacks, meanwhile, which is also a Kohler company, presents the tile maker's full range of products. Here, the space functions as a sort of library, with a blackened-steel shelving system, and mosaic flooring that highlights the tiles as they might be used in customers' own homes.

Kohler / Ann Sacks

Kohler / Ann Sacks 111

LVMH Corporate Offices

New York, NY
2011

French fashion and luxury-goods group LVMH commissioned this trio of wall reliefs to mark the entry points of its corporate offices in New York City. All three pieces share the same overall design—a gridded, multilevel installation based on the circular quatrefoil motif of the signature Louis Vuitton pattern, rendered at various scales. Each was crafted in a different material, with the wood, plaster, and polished-metal versions used to differentiate one floor from another in the office's elevator lobbies. This, in turn, eases wayfinding while also providing a strong brand identity.

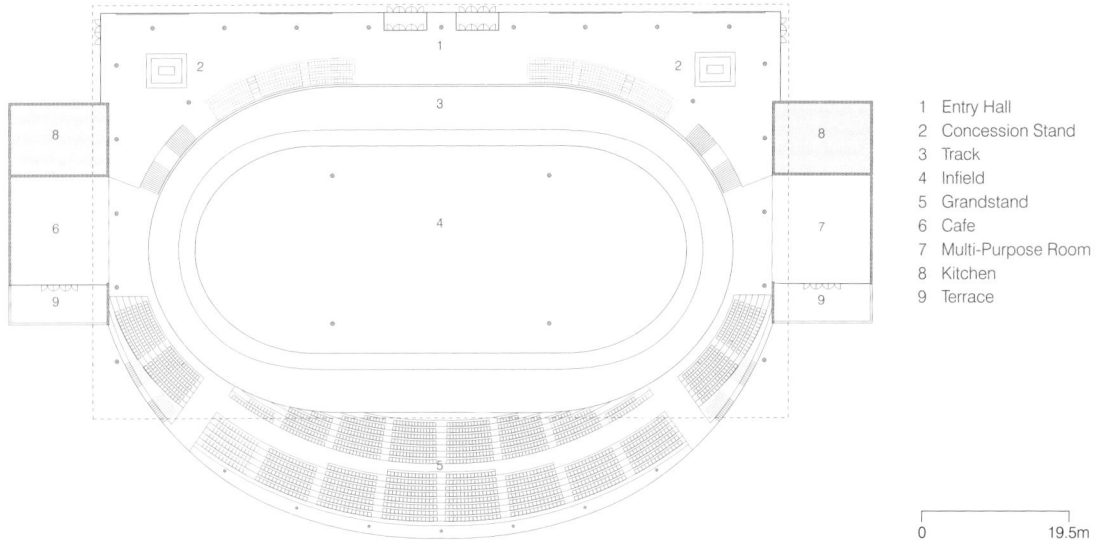

Grandstand Floor Plan

1 Entry Hall
2 Concession Stand
3 Track
4 Infield
5 Grandstand
6 Cafe
7 Multi-Purpose Room
8 Kitchen
9 Terrace

New York Velodrome

New York, NY
2009

VoNYC Inc.—a privately funded non-profit promoting track cycling in New York City—commissioned a design concept and feasibility study for this 3000-seat, 10,200-square-meter multi-use building, which combines athletic facilities with retail space, a cafe, a community center, exhibition galleries, public art, offices, locker rooms, and pre-function areas. Designed for a variety of cycling competitions, the Velodrome's 200-meter track surrounds a 2040-square-meter infield that can be used for other sports, concerts, film screenings, and conferences. A continuous glass curtain wall surrounds the track and seating areas, defining the space and allowing the public to look in, and sports spectators to gaze out. The wooden track and its structure sit like sculptures within this glass box, while a green roof with solar panels tops the building, designed to achieve LEED Gold certification.

Ogilvy Montreal

Montreal, QC
2014

This feasibility study considers the renovation and rebranding of a historic 25,550-square-meter department store in Montreal's heart, including a 4650-square-meter addition adjacent to the original 1896 building. The proposal weaves the 21st century into the 19th, connecting all six floors across both buildings, modernizing and activating the original while embracing its heritage and sense of place. Using architectural innovation to create inviting destinations, the scheme centers on a new atrium containing primary vertical circulation as well as the 'Digital Concierge'—a six-story LED-wrapped column that serves as both art and wayfinding signage. A massive contemporary skylight caps the atrium, infusing the once-dark interiors with daylight and attracting customers to higher floors. This glass structure projects across the rooftop and beyond the historic building's façade, creating an illuminated beacon, an icon in both the streetscape and the skyline.

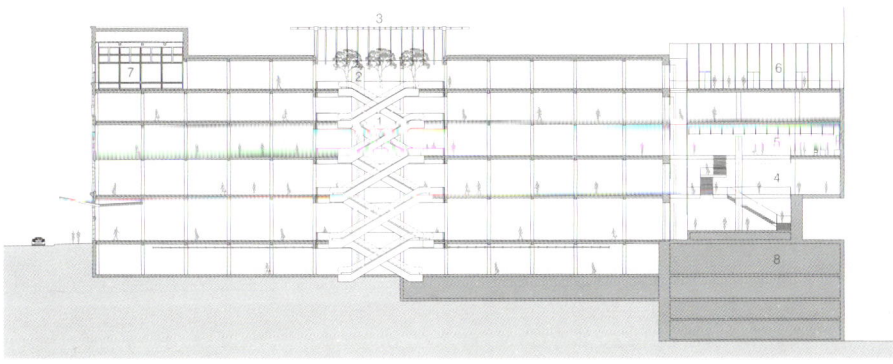

1 New Atrium
2 Digital Concierge
3 New Skylight
4 Men's Townhouse
5 Brasserie
6 Terrace
7 Tudor Room
8 Parking

0 9.7m

Section

Ogilvy Montreal 121

Fifth Floor Plan

1. New Atrium
2. Digital Concierge
3. Designer Footwear Salon
4. Contemporary Footwear Salon
5. Cafe / Event Space
6. Kitchen
7. Tudor Room
8. The Apartment
9. Terrace
10. Personal Shopping
11. Market
12. Back of House

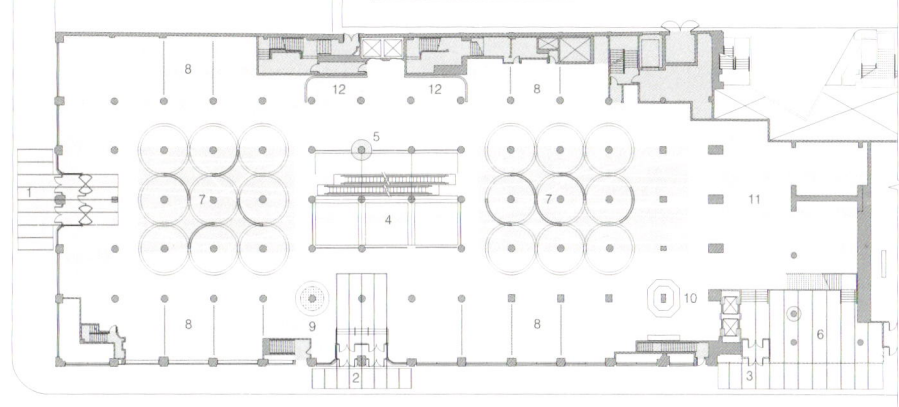

Ground Floor Plan

1. Sainte-Catherine Street Entrance
2. de la Montagne Street Entrance
3. Men's Townhouse Entrance
4. New Atrium
5. Digital Concierge
6. Men's Townhouse
7. Handbags / Leather Hall
8. Vendor Shops
9. Florist
10. Patisserie
11. Jewelry & Watches
12. Eyewear

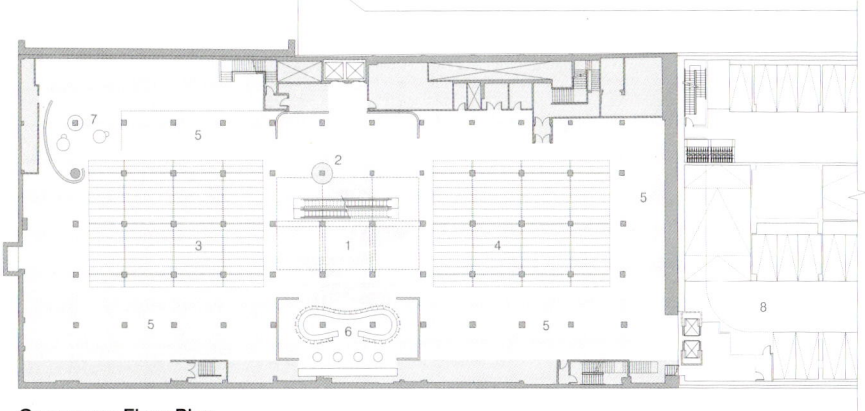

Concourse Floor Plan

1. New Atrium
2. Digital Concierge
3. Color Pavilion
4. Skincare Pavilion
5. Vender Shops
6. Juice Bar / Grab & Go
7. Beauty Services
8. Valet Parking

0   19.5m

Ogilvy Montreal

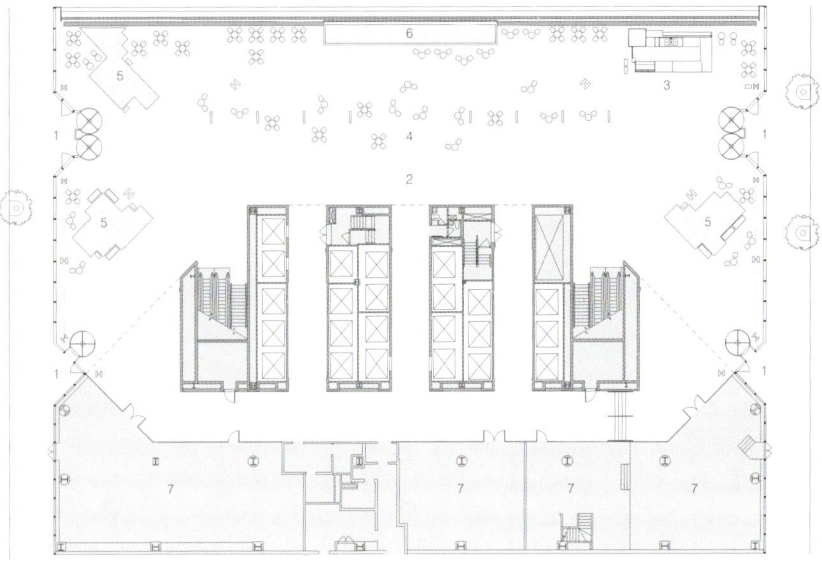

Floor Plan

1 Entry
2 Public Arcade
3 Cafe
4 Seating Area
5 Bamboo Planters
6 Fountain
7 Retail

0   9.7m

Park Avenue Plaza Public Atrium

New York, NY
2015

This redesign of a prominent Midtown Manhattan office tower's 2600-square-meter public atrium and lobby lets the building live up to the architectural pedigree of its neighborhood, which includes such modernist icons as the Seagram Building. The new scheme centers on a dramatic glass colonnade composed of eight sculptural, round-edged piers, each nine meters high, one meter wide, and 15 centimeters thick. This colonnade pulls the public in, making a path through the space, providing places to gather and offering rhythm and order. The columns also encourage spontaneity and a variety of interactions, with movable seating and a free-flowing plan allowing for multiple uses. Art, sculpture, music, digital media, and a central water feature create diverse experiences, while a continuous green wall and bamboo planters suggest an urban Eden.

Park Avenue Plaza Public Atrium

Park Avenue Plaza Public Atrium

Rocket Dog Brands Corporate Headquarters

Los Angeles, CA
2012

Occupying the second and third floors of a corner building in Los Angeles's fashion district, this 1020-square-meter space provides executive offices, design studios, and a West Coast showroom for the multi-brand footwear company. Core to the scheme is the third-floor courtyard—accessible from all sides and flanked by the design studio and a cafe—which offers natural light and fresh air as well as a central gathering place. The third floor also houses the CEO's office, while the second contains additional workspace and the showroom. A dramatic steel-and-marble staircase connects the two floors, leading from reception to the courtyard. Selected to evoke the beach, in particular nearby Malibu, the palette features distressed oak and glass in the offices, with teak-and-steel lattice enhancing the courtyard's plaster walls.

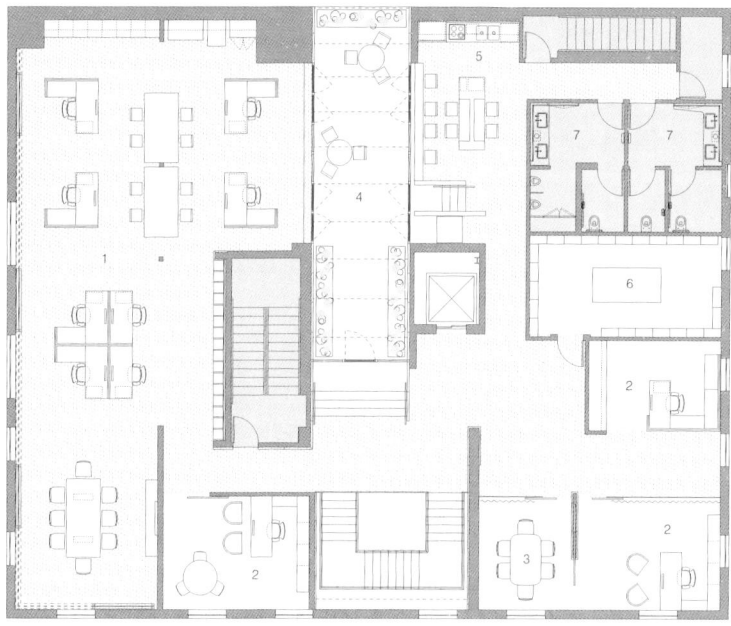

Upper Level Floor Plan
1. Design Studio
2. Office
3. Conference Room
4. Courtyard
5. Cafe
6. Library
7. Washroom

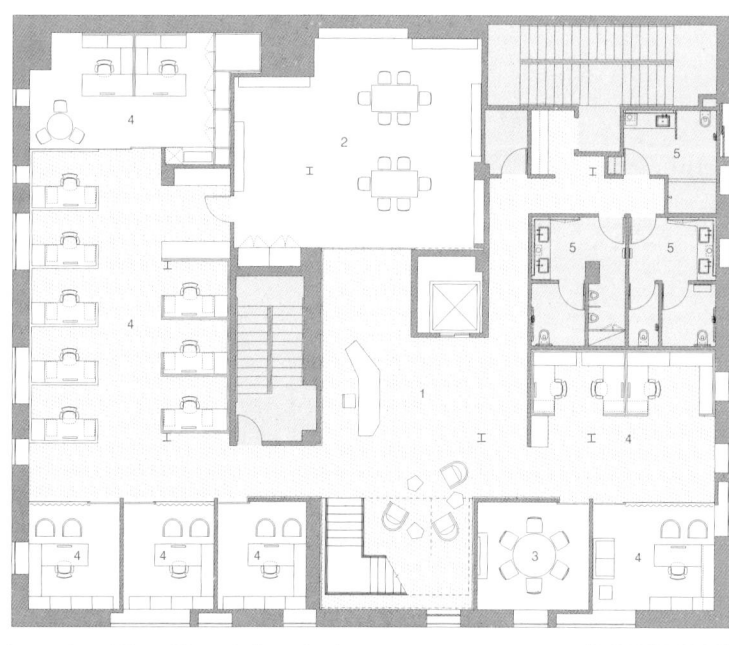

Lower Level Floor Plan
1. Reception Area
2. Showroom
3. Conference Room
4. Office / Open Plan
5. Washroom

0   4.8m

Rocket Dog Brands Corporate Headquarters

Rocket Dog Brands Corporate Headquarters

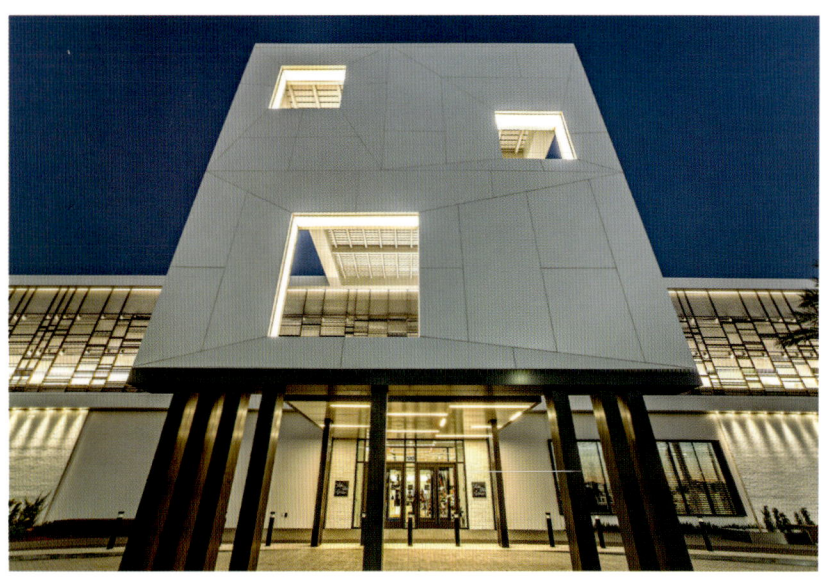

Saks Fifth Avenue

Sarasota, FL
2014

San Juan, PR
2014

Naples, FL
2009

Boca Raton, FL
2006

Beverly Hills, CA
2006

Part of a long relationship with Saks Fifth Avenue, this series of stores represents a new generation of shopping environments, one designed to emphasize the brand's 90-year heritage as an iconic luxury brand while simultaneously demonstrating its focus on the future. Ground-up projects in San Juan, Puerto Rico, and Sarasota, FL, as well as renovations of locations in Beverly Hills and South Florida, prove particularly emblematic. The San Juan and Sarasota stores feature bold façades inspired by mid-20th-century tropical modernism. Plant-covered living stonewalls at ground level give way to glazing shaded by bronze-toned *brise-soleil* above, creating a striking and iconic brand profile. Inside each location, natural sunlight gently filters through the *brise-soleil* into the store's most special spaces, including a sumptuous cafe and private-shopping suite.

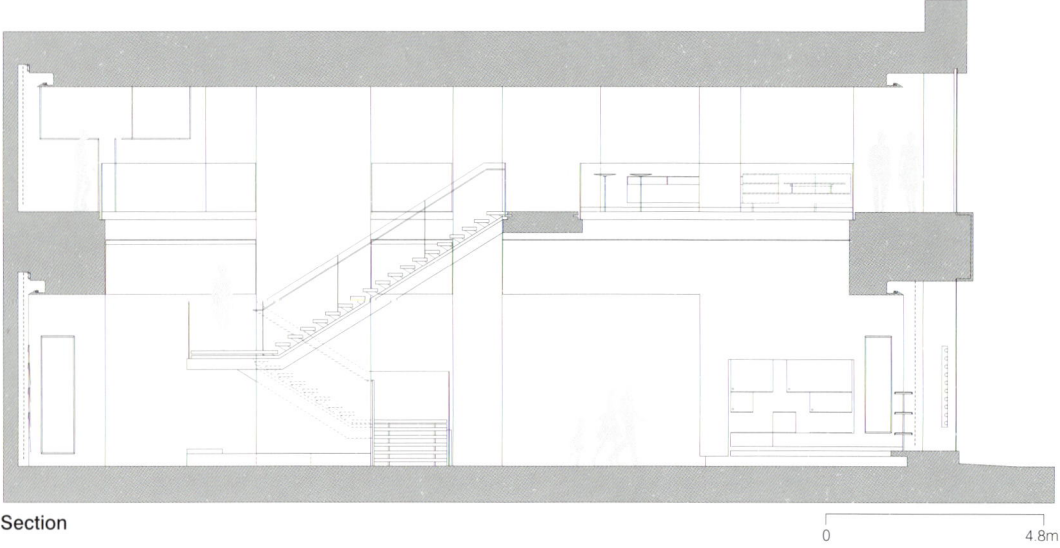

Section
0   4.8m

Salvatore Ferragamo

Fifth Avenue Flagship, New York, NY
2003
Manhasset, NY
2002

The flagship store is the central element of a multi-year collaboration with the Italian fashion house that resulted in new locations across the US. The design of this 1900-square-meter, bi-level flagship on Manhattan's Fifth Avenue inaugurated a new generation of stateside Salvatore Ferragamo stores. The flagship seamlessly melds two existing retail spaces across a pair of prominent buildings, creating a singularly grand Ferragamo environment. Containing men's and women's collections, state-of-the-art fitting rooms, a custom-footwear atelier and a gallery, the space draws customers in with enticing views down its bays, and such dramatic features as a wood, stone, and glass staircase that wraps a monolithic stone column. This terminates in a bridge connecting the store's east and west sides, leading to the men's footwear salon in a glass-enclosed aerie overlooking Fifth Avenue.

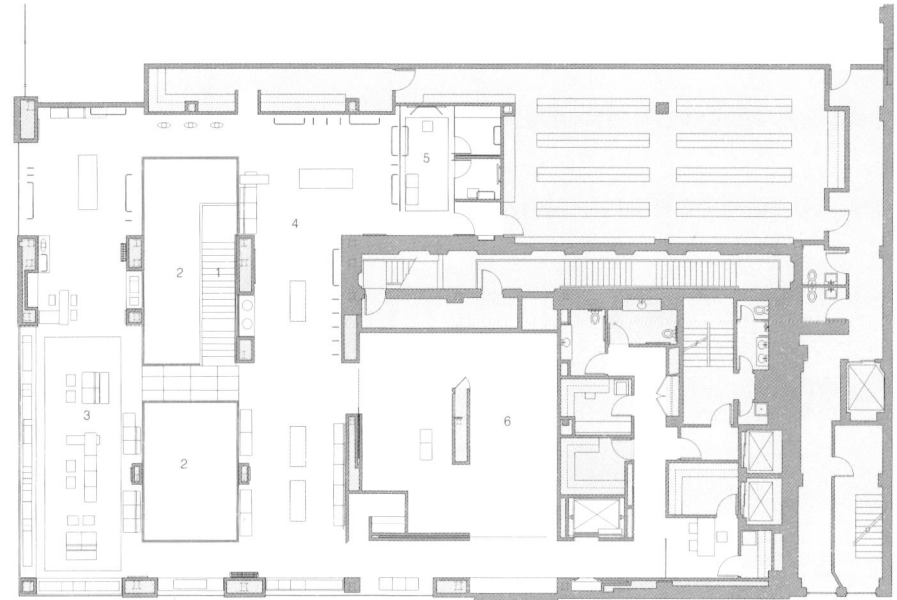

Second Floor Plan

1 Stair
2 Open to Below
3 Men's Footwear
4 Men's Apparel
5 Fitting Area
6 Gallery

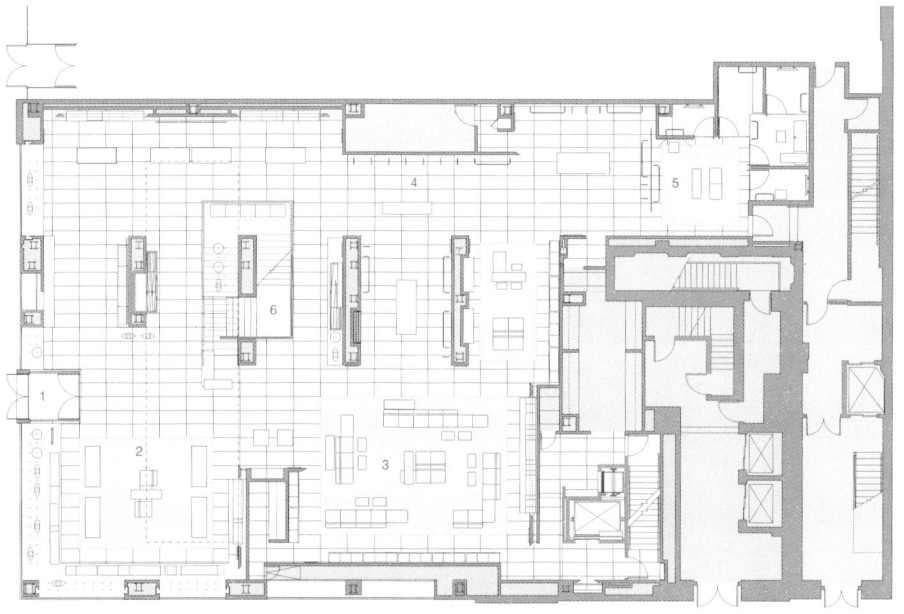

Ground Floor Plan

1 Entry
2 Handbags
3 Women's Footwear
4 Women's Apparel
5 Fitting Area
6 Stair

Floor Plan

1 Hotel Entrance
2 Mix
3 Courtyard
4 Cafe
5 Retail

0 — 9.7m

The Breakers Palm Beach Retail Shops

Palm Beach, FL
2008

Reimagining the glass-enclosed central loggia of The Breakers Palm Beach, this new master plan for the property's retail courtyard elevates and expands the shopping experience at the historic Italian Renaissance–style hotel. The concept includes a fully realized fashion-jewelry boutique called The Mix, and the development of additional branded boutiques for clothing, swimwear, and footwear. These elements enhance the guest experience, generate significant revenue, and establish The Breakers as a retail destination for affluent locals, benefiting both retail and dining venues. Freestanding at the courtyard's focal point, The Mix serves as a beacon. Its four sides of 4-meter-high, classically inspired glass arches, and unique, vertical, eye-level window displays show the jewelry off to maximum effect, especially at night, when the store's glowing windows become a major draw.

The Breakers Palm Beach Retail Shops

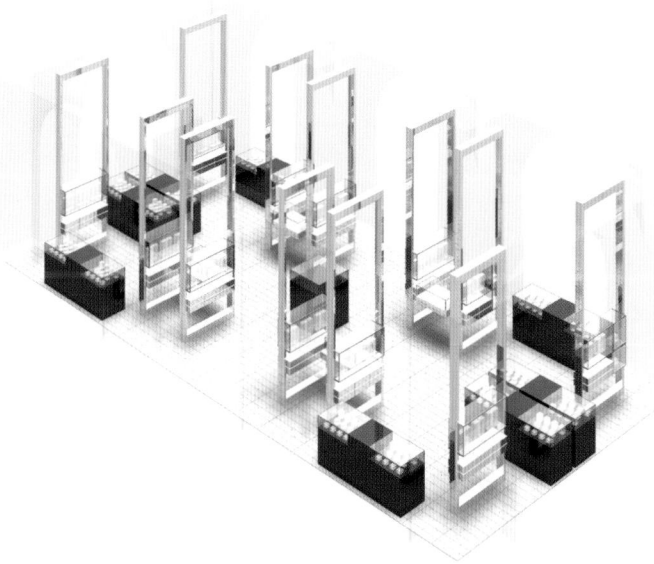

The Breakers Palm Beach Retail Shops

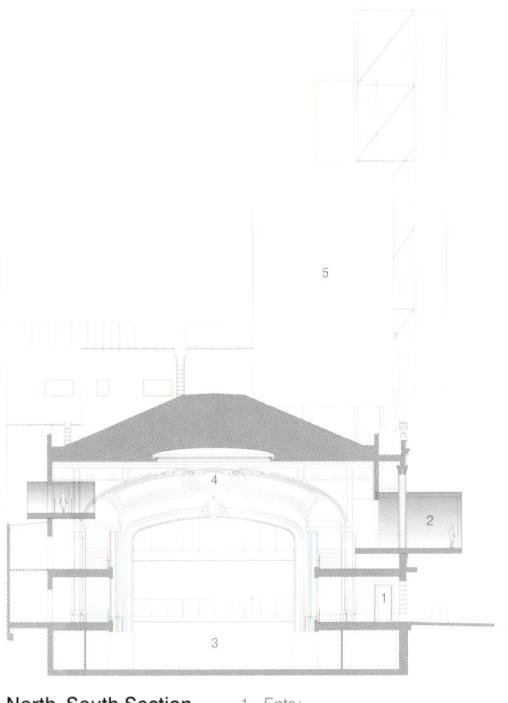
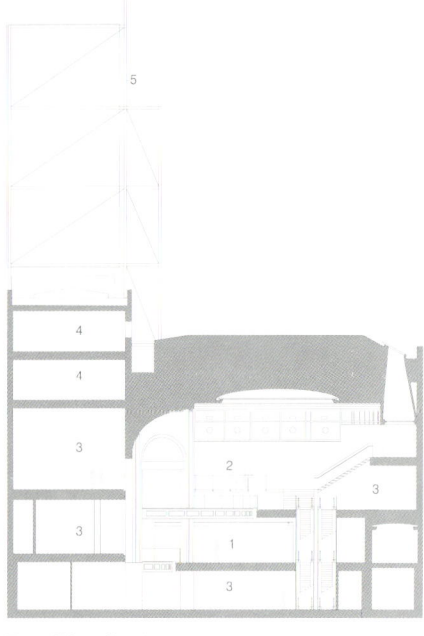

North–South Section
1 Entry
2 Glass Marquee
3 Retail
4 Historic Proscenium
5 Schematic Signage Superstructure

East–West Section
1 Entrance Beyond
2 Glass Marquee Beyond
3 Retail
4 Office (Former Flyloft)
5 Schematic Signage Superstructure

Times Square Adaptive Reuse

New York, NY
2005

The streetwear label Eckō Unltd. commissioned an extensive feasibility study to redevelop Manhattan's historic Times Square Theater, the only Broadway playhouse not yet repurposed by The New 42nd Street, an organization overseen by New York's Empire State Development authority. The study examines the adaptive reuse of the theater, considering its conversion into a flagship retail space and what Eckō calls an 'urban youth epicenter.' The proposal's most compelling feature is its reinterpretation of the marquees that once lined the street; to preserve the landmarked limestone façade and simultaneously advertise the building's new use, an occupiable glass box was designed to project through the building's colonnade and over the sidewalk. Inside the building, the auditorium becomes a grand, multi-level retail space delicately woven into the preserved historic structure and soaring proscenium.

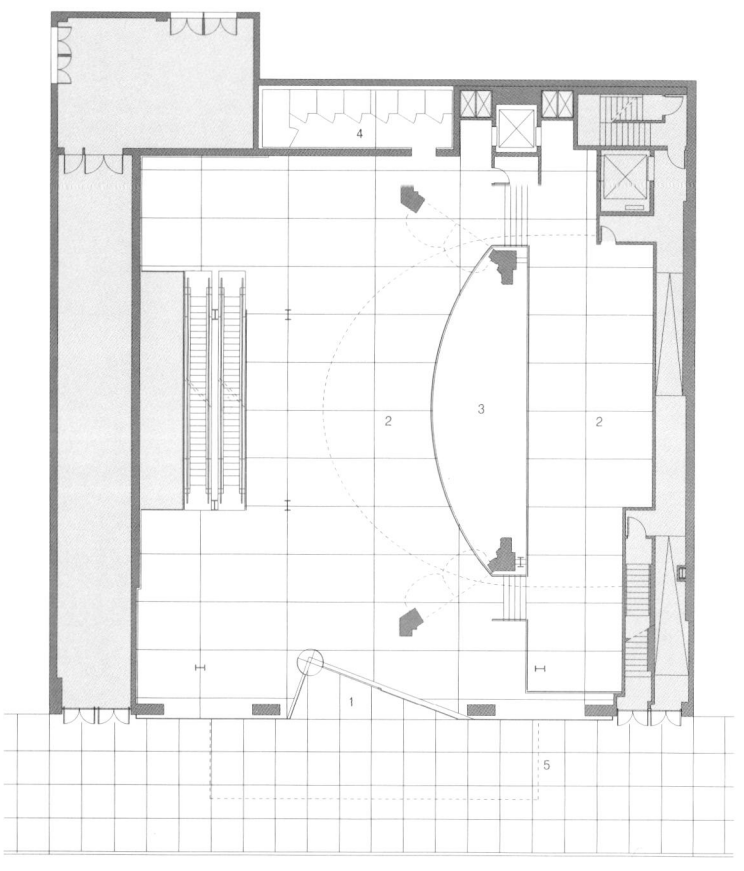

Ground Floor Plan
1. Entry
2. Retail
3. Open to Below
4. Fitting Room Complex
5. Glass Marquee Above

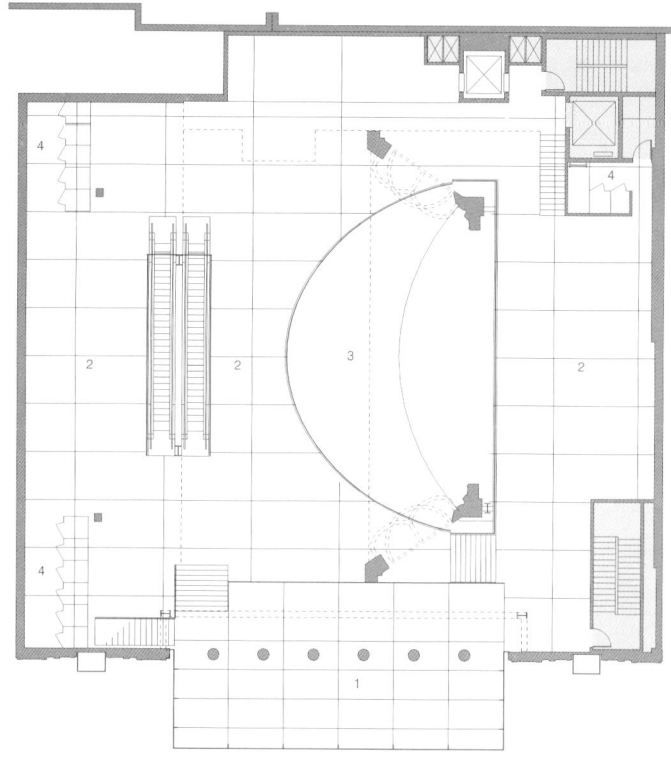

Second Floor Plan
1. Glass Marquee
2. Retail
3. Open to Below
4. Fitting Room Complex

0   9.8m

Times Square Adaptive Reuse

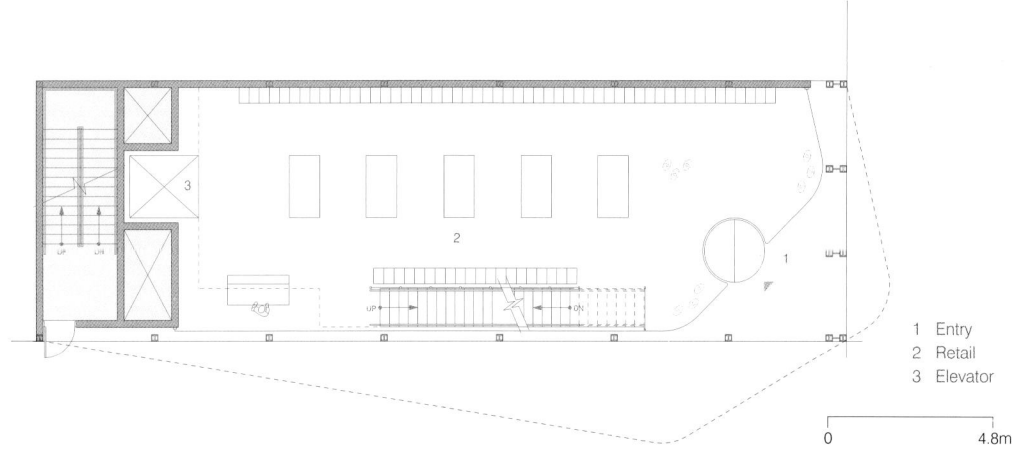

Ground Floor Plan

1 Entry
2 Retail
3 Elevator

Times Square Commercial Development

New York, NY
2014

The feasibility study for this site, located at the north end of Manhattan's Times Square, envisioned a new, single-tenant, 740-square-meter flagship location for a large retail brand. Offering four stories of retail space and one floor of offices and showrooms on what is currently an underutilized, single-level site, the new structure maximizes the allowable floor-area ratio (FAR), as well as retail square footage, visible street frontage, and space for LED billboard advertising on the building's façade—an iconic element and a prime revenue driver of any new Times Square development.

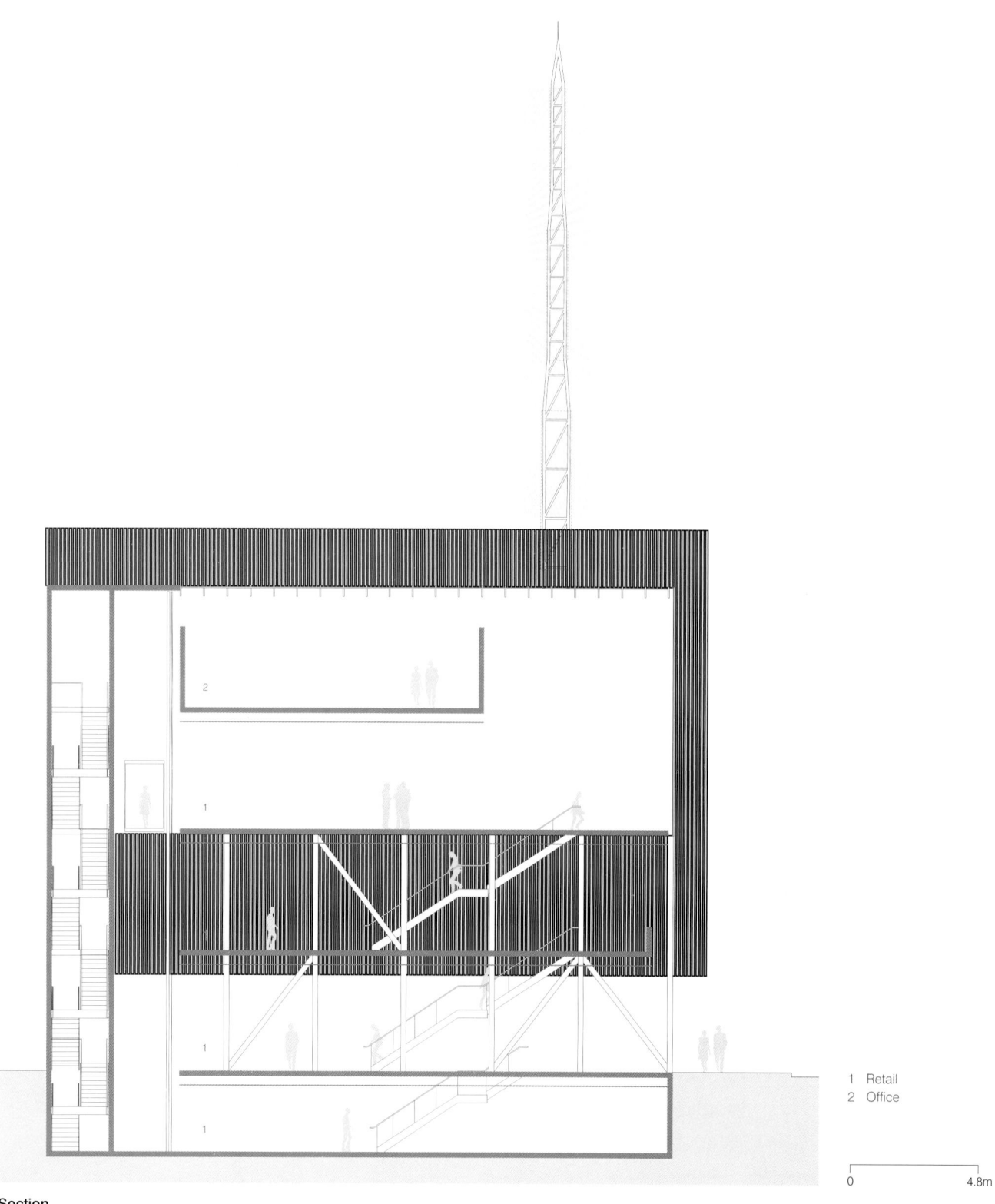

Section

1 Retail
2 Office

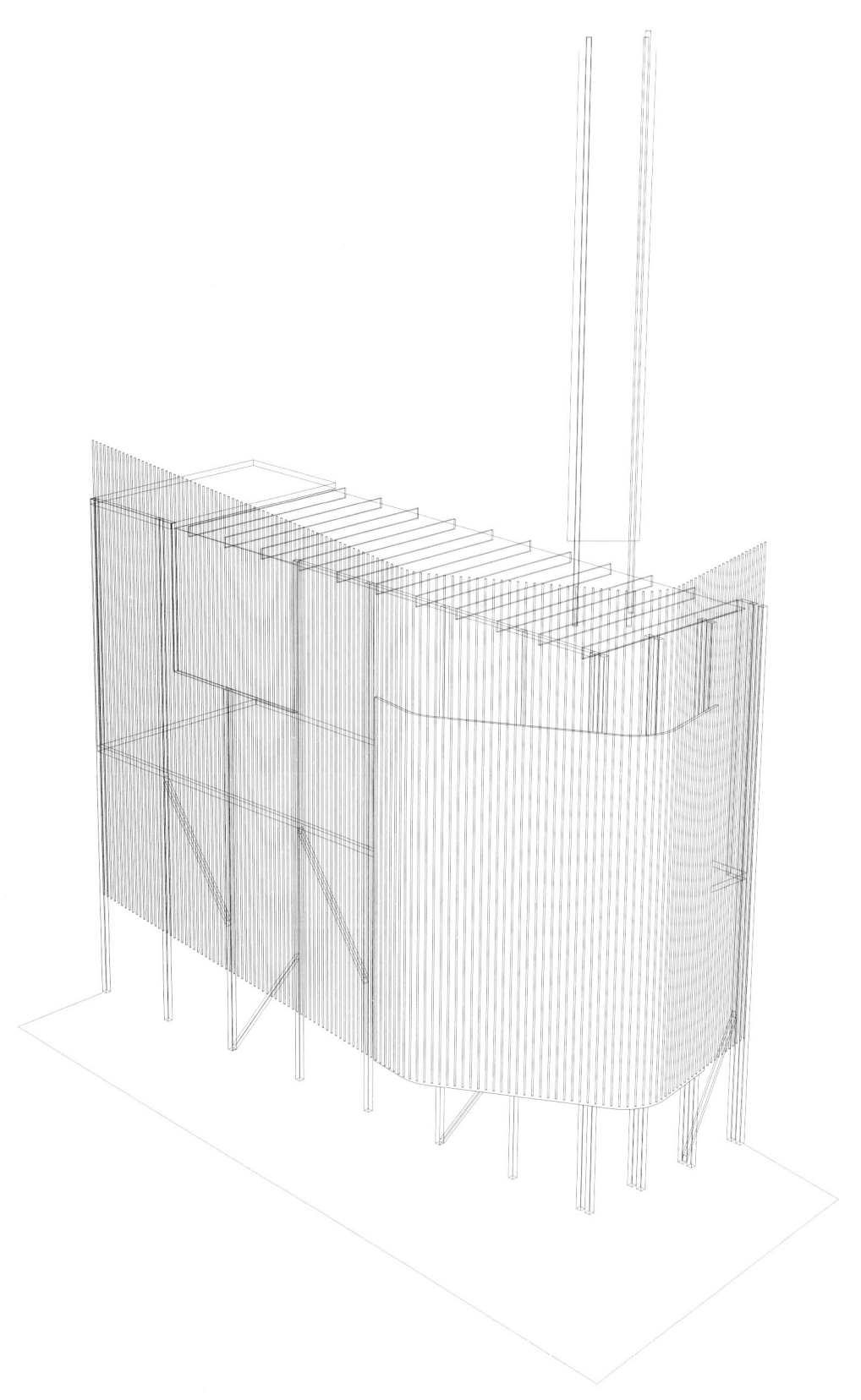

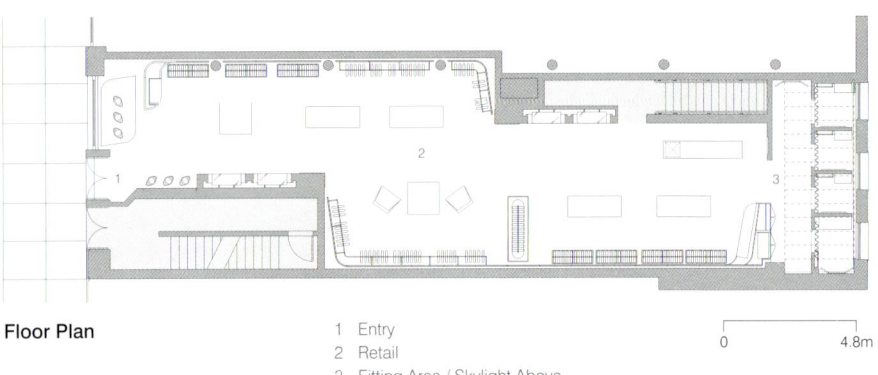

Floor Plan

1 Entry
2 Retail
3 Fitting Area / Skylight Above

0   4.8m

TSE Soho

New York, NY
2008

The design for this downtown Manhattan outlet of the high-fashion cashmere label TSE was born out of the aesthetic of a historic, quintessentially gritty Soho loft, now newly outfitted with modern, luxurious finishes. The boutique retains the brick walls, oak floors, and exposed ductwork and piping of the original raw space, juxtaposing them with refined, highly lacquered, soft-white wall panels whose curving shape creates a ribbon effect throughout the store. The smooth finishes of these panels both contrast with and complement the rich, intricate textures of the cashmere. Lightweight display fixtures—made of gently arched, satin-finished stainless-steel bars—hang from the ceiling or stand in front of walls, giving the sense that the clothing is floating above the floor or in front of the lacquered panels, rather than simply hanging.

TSE Soho

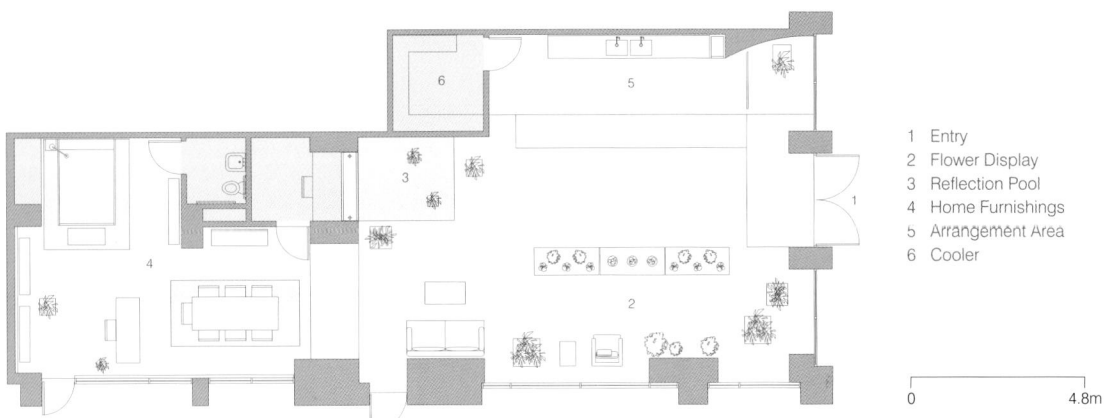

Bloom Floor Plan

1 Entry
2 Flower Display
3 Reflection Pool
4 Home Furnishings
5 Arrangement Area
6 Cooler

W Hotel Lexington Avenue

Bliss 49 + Spa Suites, New York, NY
2005
Bloom Flowers, New York, NY
2000

This floor-through renovation of Starwood Hotels & Resorts' original W Hotel encompasses an expansive 2300 square meters, including a spa, a gym, men's and women's lounge and locker facilities, three retail spaces, 11 guest rooms, and four spa suites specifically designed for guests focusing their stays on health and wellness. On the northeast corner of the street level, a satellite of the well-known New York florist Bloom puts the theatricality of flower arranging at center stage, giving customers a window into the artistry. Adjacent to Bloom is the entry for the Bliss 49 Spa, as well as its salon and retail outlet. Just beyond lie dedicated elevators that deliver clients directly to the fourth floor, which is exclusively devoted to spa services and spa suites.

W Hotel Lexington Avenue 165

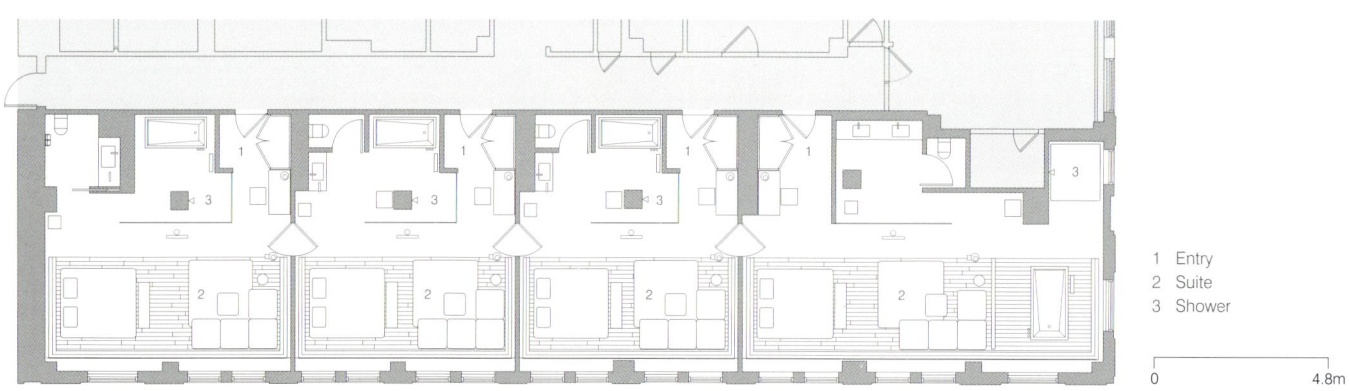

Spa Suites Floor Plan

1 Entry
2 Suite
3 Shower

0 4.8m

5 Star Hotel and Residences

New York, NY
2006

This mixed-use project near Lower Manhattan's historic South Street Seaport comprises a 50-story condominium tower and a six-floor base structure housing a five-star hotel. Creating an intimate, luxurious arrival experience, a unique porte-cochère allows guests and residents to drive through the building, removing them from street and pedestrian traffic. From the porte-cochère, the condominium lobby sits to the east, and the hotel's lobby, restaurant and bar to the west, all with 6-meter-high ceilings, and façades sheathed in glass. Atop the hotel, a landscaped terrace includes a gym, a yoga studio, and a lap pool perched on the building's edge, overlooking the Brooklyn Bridge, while the tower's rooftop features a swimming pool enclosed by a 6-meter-high glass wind screen. The condominiums' loft-like floor plans emphasize expansive river and harbor views.

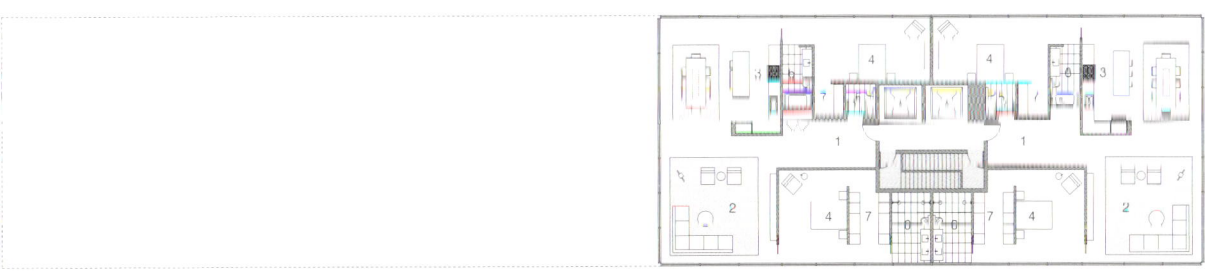

Two Unit Floor Plan

1 Gallery
2 Living Room
3 Kitchen / Dining
4 Bedroom
5 Powder Room
6 Bathroom
7 Walk in Closet

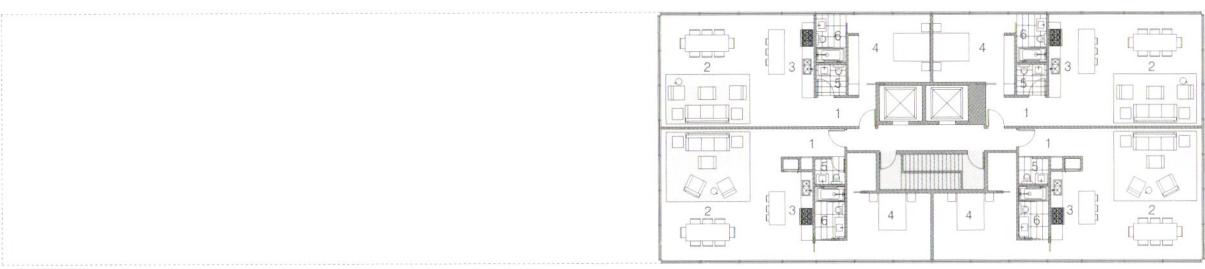

Four Unit Floor Plan

1 Entry
2 Living / Dining
3 Kitchen
4 Bedroom
5 Powder Room
6 Bathroom

Typical Hotel Floor Plan

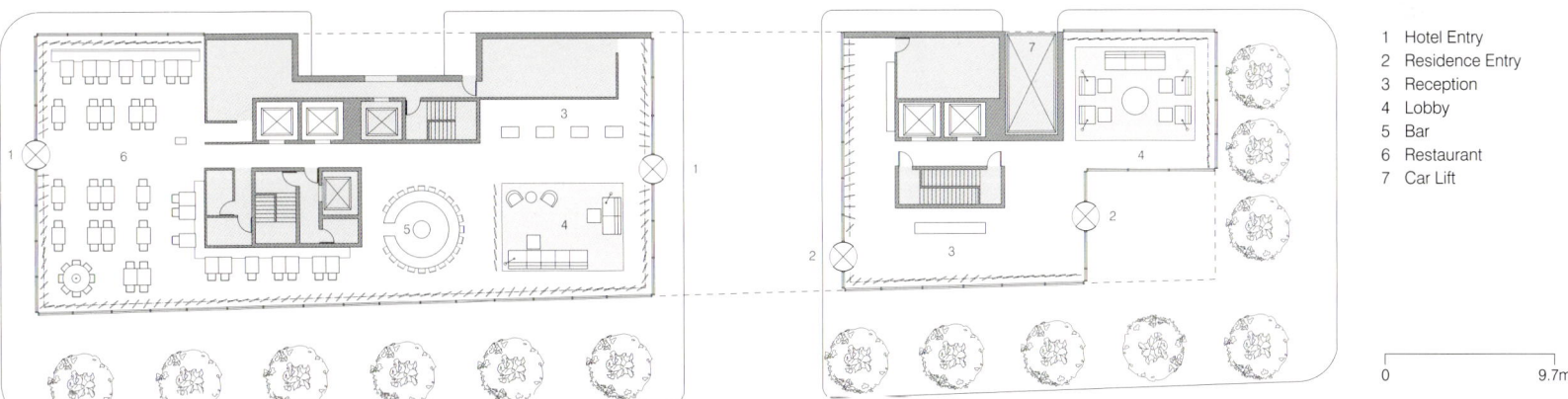

Ground Floor Plan

1 Hotel Entry
2 Residence Entry
3 Reception
4 Lobby
5 Bar
6 Restaurant
7 Car Lift

0   9.7m

5 Star Hotel and Residences   171

1 Juice Bar
2 Yoga Studio
3 Gym
4 Lap Pool
5 Terrace / Garden

0   9.8m

Roof Plan

5 Star Hotel and Residences

Site Plan

1 Entry Plaza
2 Lobby
3 Retail Pavilion

1200 New Hampshire Avenue NW

Washington, DC
2012

Near the Washington, DC, neighborhood of Dupont Circle, the addition of a new entry plaza, lobby entry and, most prominently, a sparkling glass retail pavilion transforms a 35-year-old brick office building. Carefully inserted into the foreground of the existing structure, the 929-square-meter pavilion is clad in custom-made, 6.7-meter-high glass panels. These panels feature a patterned, mirrored interlayer that both reflects the streetscape—including a small park across the street—and allows for views into the new space, now occupied by a bank and a future television studio. The design of the glass and its uninterrupted, mullion-free installation abstract the pavilion's mass, and shifting natural light creates continuous changes in its appearance. Inside, the lobby combines a crystal-clear, low-iron glass façade, oil-quenched-bronze walls, flame-finished granite and polished quartzite.

1200 New Hampshire Avenue NW   179

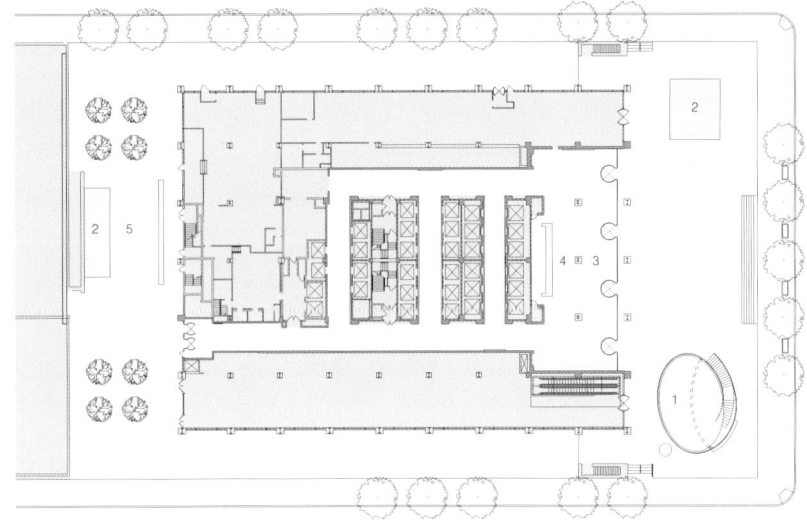

Site Plan

1 Concourse Level Courtyard
2 Fountain
3 Lobby
4 Reception
5 Fisher Park

0   19.5m

1345 Avenue of the Americas

New York, NY
2014

This project calls for the reinvigoration of the 50-story Midtown Manhattan office tower at 1345 Avenue of the Americas. The owners sought to reimagine the building's lobby, public plaza and existing underground retail and commercial space, which was inaccessible from the street. An iconic architectural feature rebrands the property, replacing existing plaza fountains and serving both as a beacon for passersby and as a welcoming entry point to a newly activated underground space. The scheme sees a monumental elliptical glass canopy supported at an angle by an arching beam across the entrance. This lens-like oculus covers the similarly shaped sunken space, providing daylight, sky views and visual connection between the plaza above and the commercial space below.

1345 Avenue of the Americas

RESIDENTIAL WORK

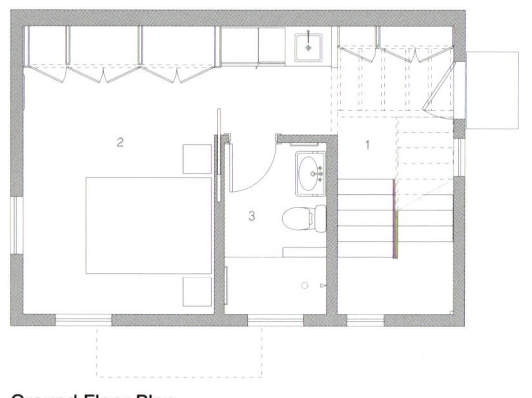

Ground Floor Plan

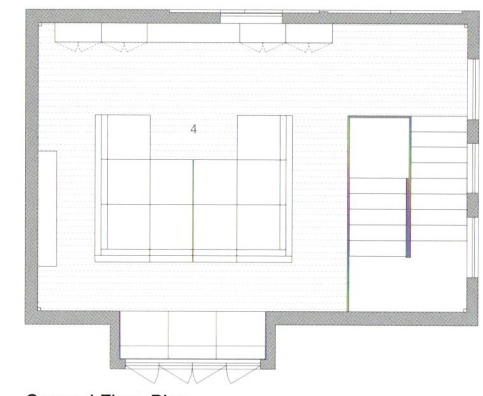

Second Floor Plan

1 Stair Hall
2 Guest Room
3 Bathroom
4 Media Room

0   2.4m

Bedford Guesthouse

Bedford, NY
2010

Making new from old, this adaptive reuse project on an estate in the suburban New York village of Bedford converted a historic barn into a rustic-but-refined 74-square-meter guesthouse. The historic structure needed complete reconstruction, and the village required it to be rebuilt in its original form. To meet this challenge, the structure was painstakingly measured, then disassembled and rebuilt to carefully maintain its quirky slopes and mismatched corners. Finished with wood shingles, the barn will weather to its original silver-gray color. The two-story interior fulfills two functions, the upper level serving as a media room for weekend movie viewing, the lower containing guest entry, bedroom and bathroom. Inside, the mix of reclaimed materials includes a ceiling clad in wood repurposed from the original exterior siding.

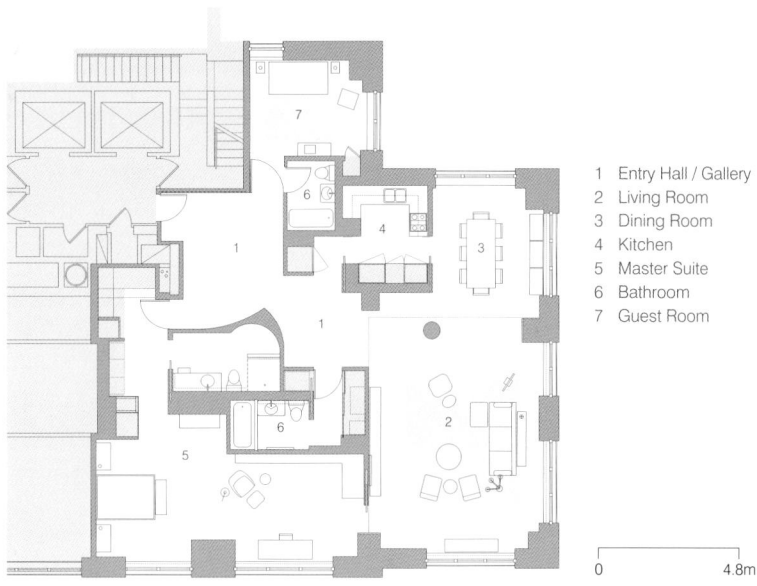

1 Entry Hall / Gallery
2 Living Room
3 Dining Room
4 Kitchen
5 Master Suite
6 Bathroom
7 Guest Room

Floor Plan

Central Park West Residence

New York, NY
2002

Designed to display the homeowner's important collection of 20th-century and contemporary photography, this two-bedroom, 190-square-meter apartment on Manhattan's Central Park West exhibits a distinct gallery-like atmosphere. In its public spaces, which comprise an entry hall and living and dining areas, creamy-gray poured-terrazzo floors and white walls combine with lighting specifically designed to highlight the artworks. In contrast, the private spaces, including the master suite, are finished in muted, natural tones. The bleached-wood floors, Venetian plaster, limestone, and French oak of these rooms create more personal, intimate environments.

Central Park West Residence

Floor Plan

1 Entry
2 Living Room
3 Kitchen / Dining
4 Bedroom
5 Plunge Bath
6 Shower
7 WC

0 — 4.8m

Cortlandt Manor Residence

Cortlandt Manor, NY
1995

Created for a contemporary-art collector, this 200-square-meter, one-bedroom home north of Manhattan serves as a personal retreat from the city. Its concept centers on four identical cubes—defined by sets of parallel brick walls—rotated in relation to each other as they line up to form a rectangular residence. Equal in size, each contains a single central function: eating, sleeping, bathing, or relaxing. Two-meter-wide glass enclosures connect the cubes, allowing square footage to expand in either direction—to create a larger living space, for instance. The house sits next to a wooded landscape, but the owner's need for wall space for art took precedence over large windows capitalizing on the views. A long, tree-lined drive does take advantage of the setting, however, shielding the structure from the public and making for a dramatic reveal.

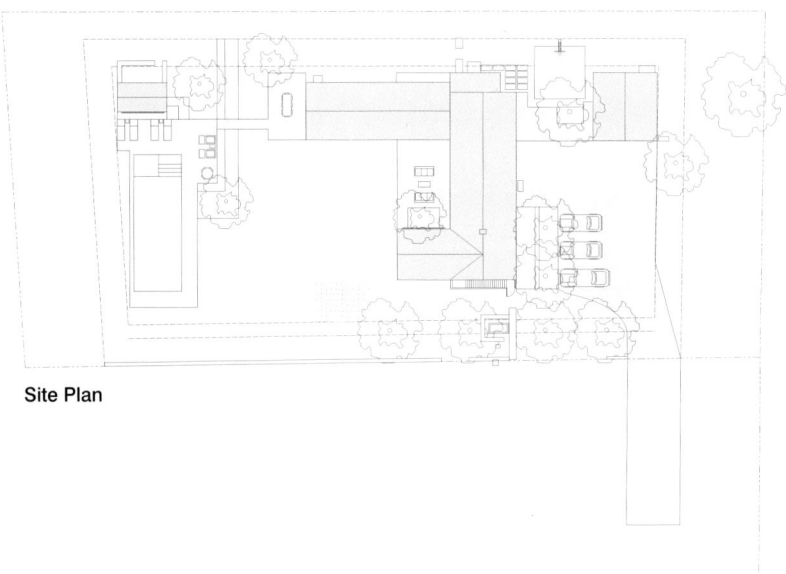

Site Plan

East Hampton Residence

Village of East Hampton, NY
2013

This 900-square-meter newly built house combines a traditional façade, inspired by its setting in the quaint village of East Hampton, with contemporary, light-filled interiors designed for 21st-century living. Formal, historic and private, the street-facing elevation displays the elegant proportions, and spare detail of Shaker architecture, while the rear proves more informal, modern, and open, its wide sliding-glass doors leading to a sun-filled backyard. Inside, natural materials and large windows visually connect this family country home to the landscape. The ground-floor great room's exposed wood rafters, open plan, and natural light—much of it from a 14-meter-long gabled skylight—continue the relaxed feeling. Upstairs, four bedrooms sit off a single hallway running the length of the house, allowing for easy transfer of light and air.

East Hampton Residence

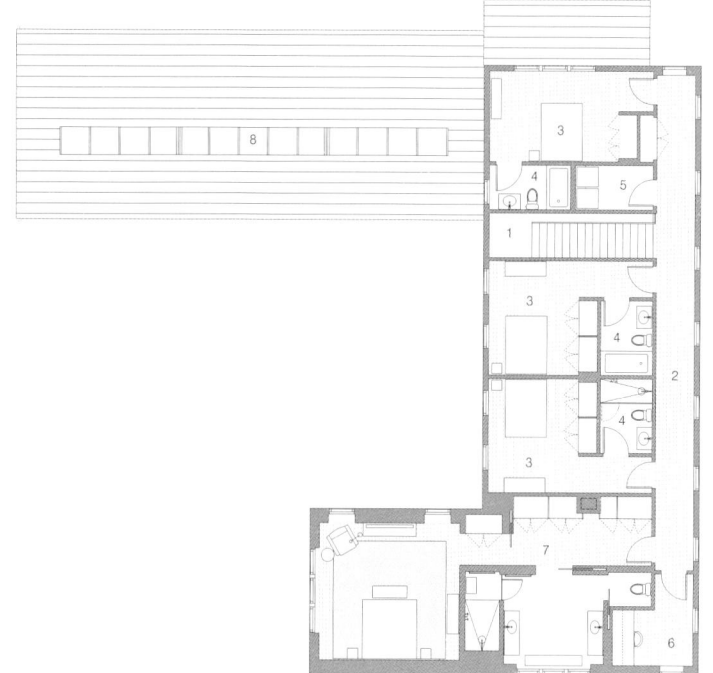

Second Floor Plan

1. Stair Hall
2. Hall
3. Bedroom
4. Bathroom
5. Laundry
6. Study
7. Master Suite
8. Skylight

Ground Floor Plan

1. Entry Hall
2. Living Room
3. Family Room
4. Kitchen
5. Pantry
6. Mud Room
7. Powder Room
8. Laundry
9. Bedroom
10. Bathroom
11. Terrace

East Hampton Residence

East Hampton Residence 209

East Hampton Residence

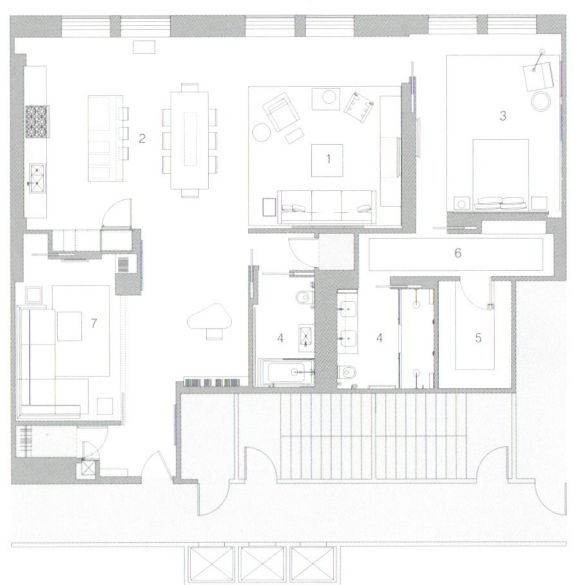

1 Living Area
2 Kitchen / Dining Area
3 Bedroom
4 Bathroom
5 Walk-in Closet
6 Dressing Area
7 Media Room

0   4.8m

Floor Plan

Greenwich Village Loft

New York, NY
2009

A study in materiality, with texture and pattern explored in virtually every surface, this project in Manhattan's Greenwich Village transformed a raw commercial space into a 160-square-meter loft comprising a master suite, a convertible media-guestroom, and a great room with an open kitchen designed for entertaining. Clad largely in stainless steel and European walnut, the kitchen centers on a French marble–topped island whose angled, mirror-polished sides reflect a fumed-oak floor and clear acrylic stools. The eclectic living area features a herringbone-patterned, warmly colored silk rug, and custom crushed-velvet sofa, and lacquered credenza. In the bedroom, an eel-skin leather headboard sits atop a celadon silk carpet, while the media-guestroom includes a mid-20th-century Italian glass pendant light and raked-plaster walls. Calacatta marble slabs and floating glass walls define the bathrooms.

Greenwich Village Loft 217

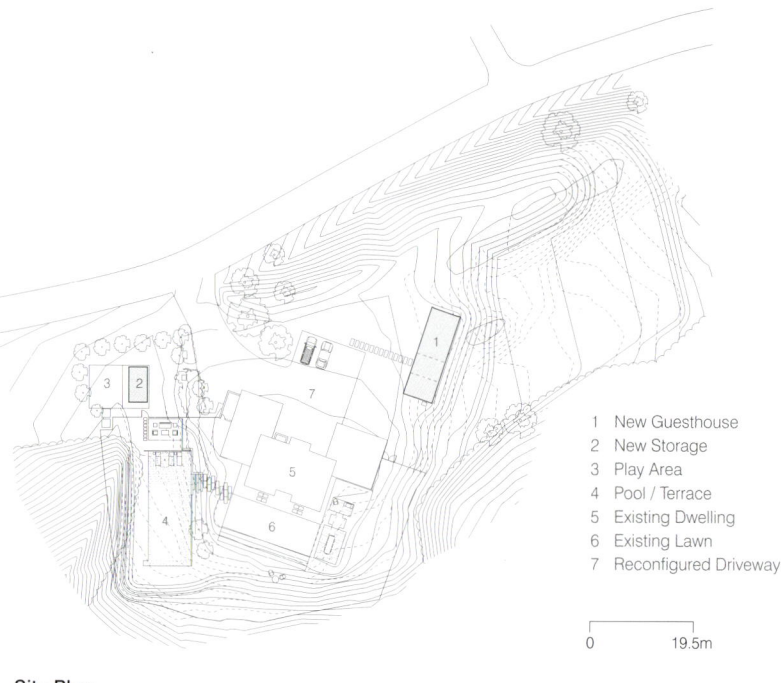

Site Plan

1 New Guesthouse
2 New Storage
3 Play Area
4 Pool / Terrace
5 Existing Dwelling
6 Existing Lawn
7 Reconfigured Driveway

0 19.5m

Hudson Guesthouse

Hudson, NY
2015

The master plan for this four-acre hillside site outside of the upstate New York town of Hudson includes a new guesthouse and pool adjacent to an existing contemporary home. The 6-by-14-meter pool takes advantage of the property's Hudson Valley views, while the guesthouse, nearly surrounded by a new meadow, forms an entry court with the main structure. A covered breezeway divides the guesthouse into two sides: one side a gym, the other a living-and-sleeping area for guests. The opening acts as a bridge between the sides, allowing for privacy as well as connection to the surrounding landscape. Clad in vertical wooden slats, the structure's simple construction, including exposed rafters and concrete flooring, features an elegant glass wall that maximizes the building's transparency and views.

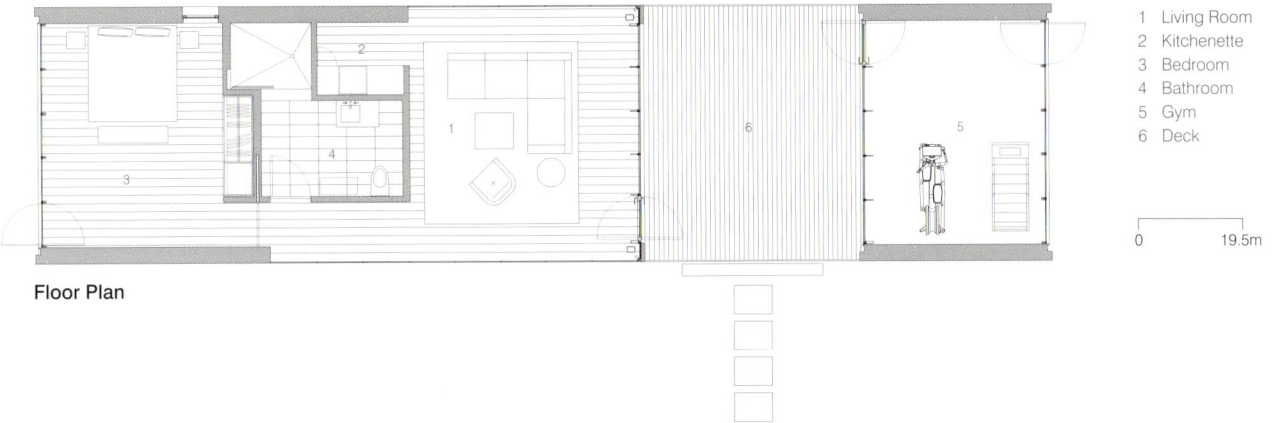

Floor Plan

1 Living Room
2 Kitchenette
3 Bedroom
4 Bathroom
5 Gym
6 Deck

0   19.5m

Hudson Guesthouse

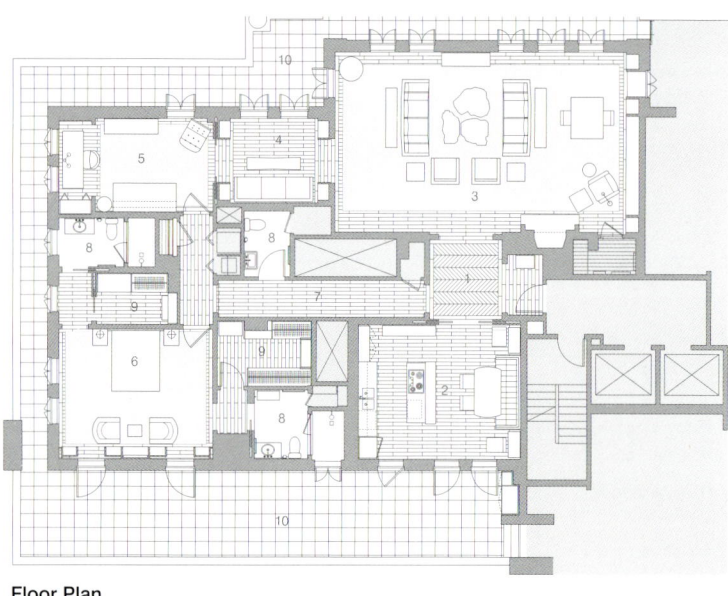

1 Foyer
2 Kitchen
3 Living Room
4 Library
5 Study
6 Bedroom
7 Gallery
8 Bathroom
9 Walk-in Closet
10 Terrace

0   4.8m

Floor Plan

London Terrace Penthouse

New York, NY
2011

Perched atop majestic London Terrace, a Depression-era development in Manhattan's Chelsea neighborhood, this 240-square-meter residence started out as a dark and claustrophobic four-bedroom apartment, emerging after a massive renovation as a spacious and light-filled one-bedroom penthouse. A simplified and largely open plan organizes the home on two axes, allowing views through its rooms and to skyline vistas beyond. A series of 22 new glass-and-steel French doors and windows replaces original small window openings, maximizing these views and allowing access to a wraparound terrace. Newly created spaces include a master suite with a bedroom and two bathrooms; an enfilade of rooms connecting the living room, library, and study; and an eat-in kitchen designed for easy entertaining. The interiors feature the clients' collection of antiques and art, as well as new and custom-created pieces and luxurious textiles.

London Terrace Penthouse

London Terrace Penthouse

Manhattan Townhouse

New York, NY
2014

The sweeping scope of this seven-story townhouse project on Manhattan's Upper East Side comprises six bedrooms; living, dining, and kitchen areas; a gym; and a subterranean indoor swimming pool, as well as a backyard and roof terrace. The homeowners purchased the historic building after its renovation and then commissioned custom interiors. Existing Italian-oak paneling set the stage for a selection of modern furniture carefully placed throughout the 840-square-meter house. Sheer draperies and muted fabrics bring a sense of calm quietude and serenity to the interiors, as does the spare quality of the overall scheme, which allows the clients' art collection—including works by Andy Warhol and Thomas Struth—to take center stage.

Floor Plans

1. Terrace
2. Guest Bedroom
3. Bathroom
4. Library
5. Master Suite
6. Living Room
7. Dining Room
8. Powder Room
9. Butler Pantry
10. Foyer
11. Office
12. Maid's Room
13. Kitchen
14. Yard

Manhattan Townhouse 235

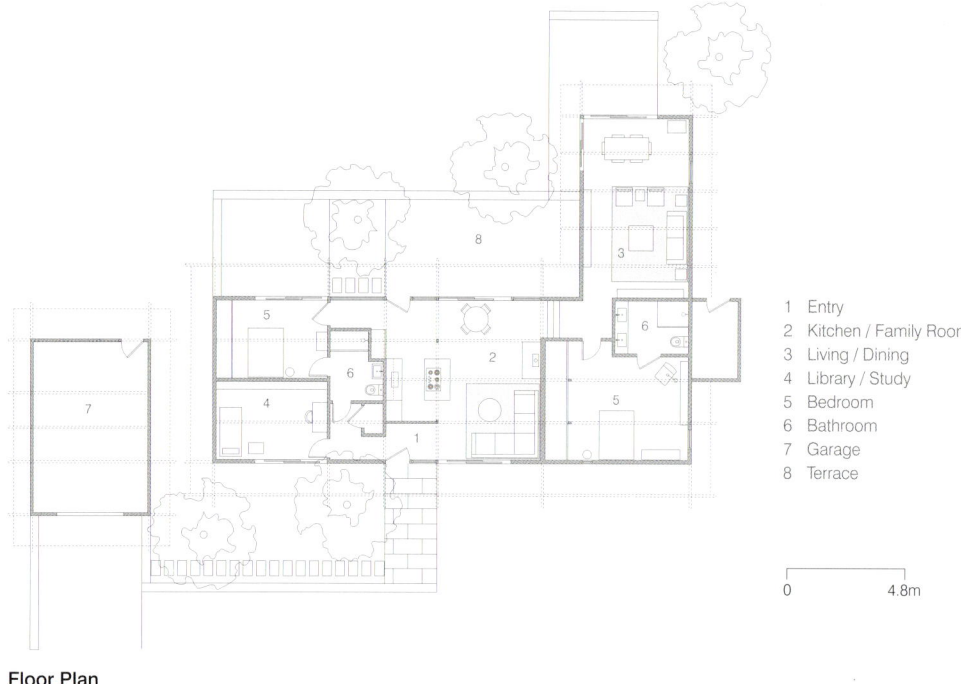

Floor Plan

1 Entry
2 Kitchen / Family Room
3 Living / Dining
4 Library / Study
5 Bedroom
6 Bathroom
7 Garage
8 Terrace

Mid Century Residence

Dutchess County, NY
2014

A sensitive restoration of a classic mid-20th-century residence in New York's Hudson Valley highlights and heightens the strong modernist lines of the 1968 home, while simultaneously adapting the two-bedroom, 610-square-meter house for contemporary living. Carefully selected furnishings comprise an era-appropriate collection of vintage pieces, including classic and rare designs by the likes of Greta Magnusson Grossman, Milo Baughman, Jens Risom, and Paul McCobb, all complemented by contemporary lighting and new custom creations. A redesign of the 7-acre property's grounds—which now prominently feature a wildflower meadow and a pool lined with slabs of native New York bluestone—completes the project.

Mid Century Residence

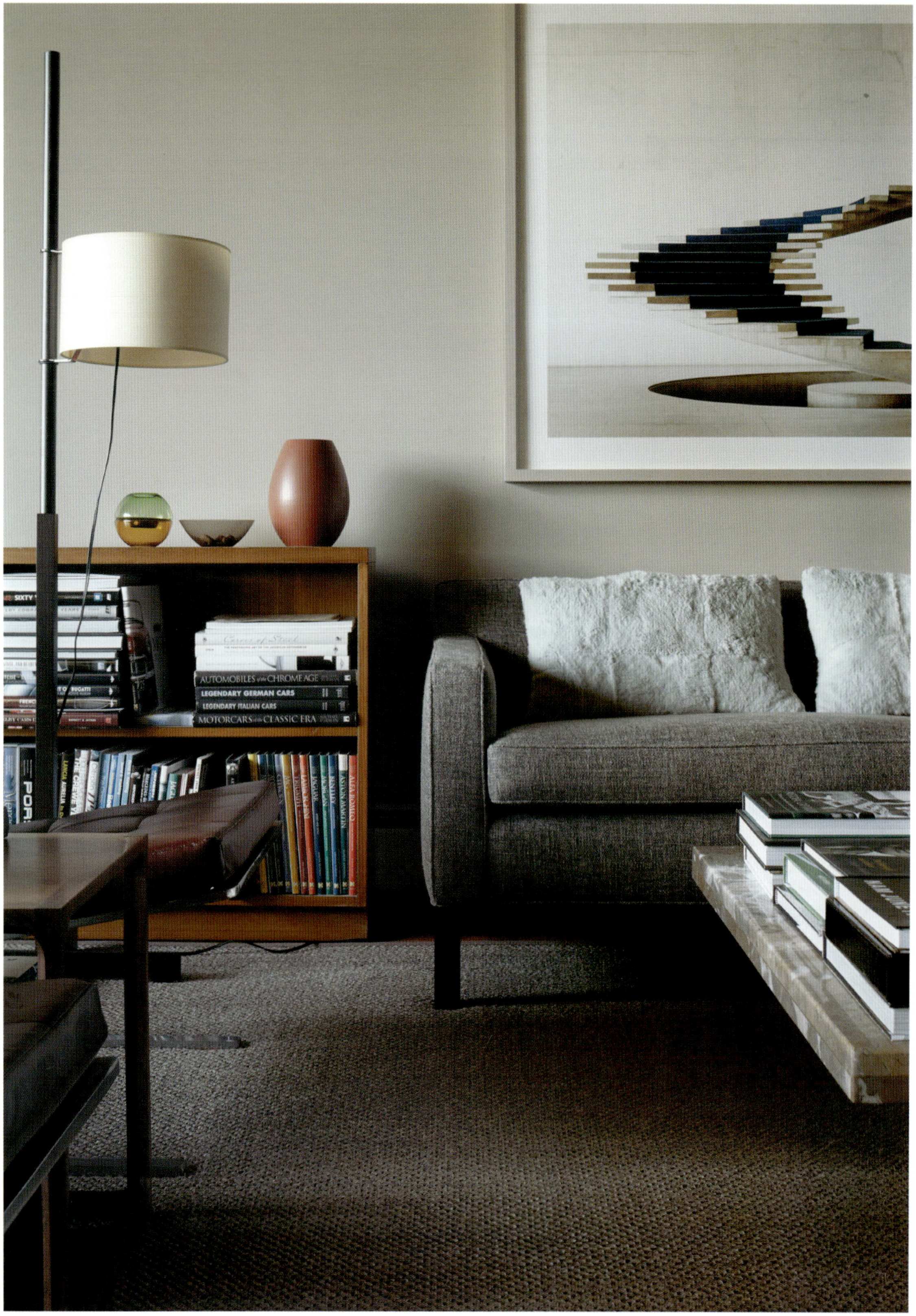
LEGENDARY GERMAN CARS
LEGENDARY ITALIAN CARS

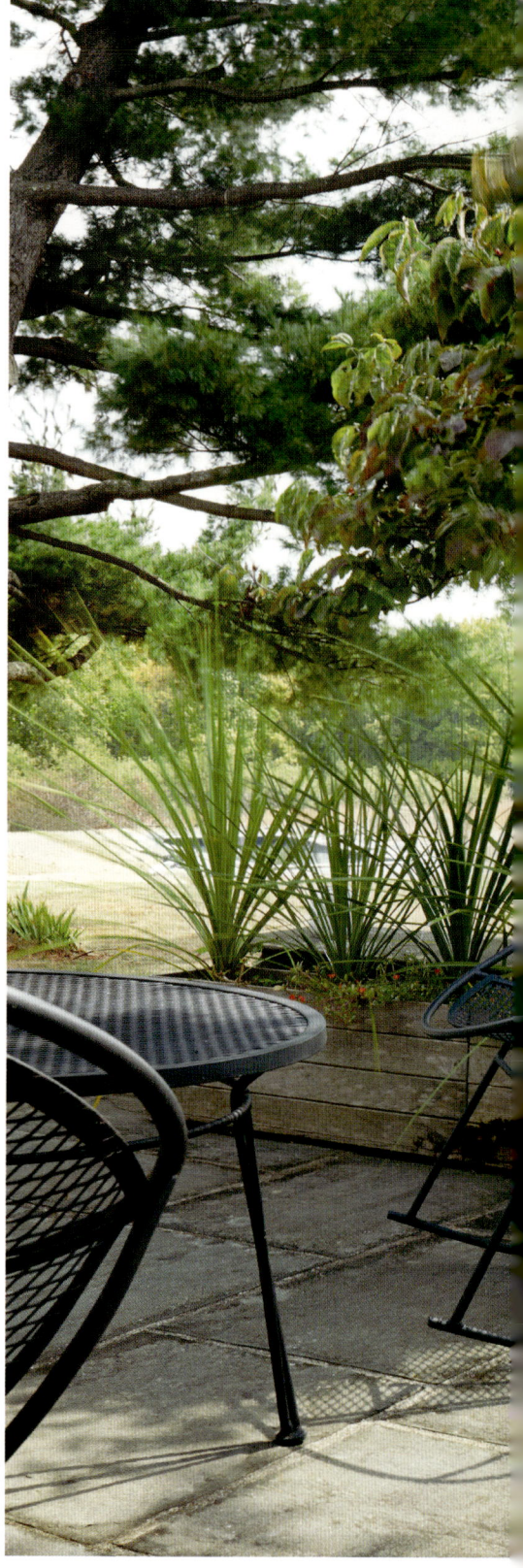

Mid Century Residence   247

Site Plan

0　　19.5m

Red Hook Residence

Red Hook, NY
2015

This 465-square-meter residence lies at the end of a long, winding drive in the Hudson Valley town of Red Hook, NY, at the edge of a meadow and surrounded by woodlands. Conceived as an intimate private residence, able to both accommodate family gatherings and entertain guests, the house is organized along a series of interconnected perpendicular axes that create sightlines to carry the eye through the interior and out into the landscape beyond. These axes also divide the home into several pavilions, each with a separate function: there's a grand entertaining pavilion, master and guest-suite pavilions, a library pavilion that converts into a second guest suite, and a garage with a loft-like, second-floor space that can be used as an additional guest apartment.

Red Hook Residence

Elevation 0 — 4.8m

Section 0 — 4.8m

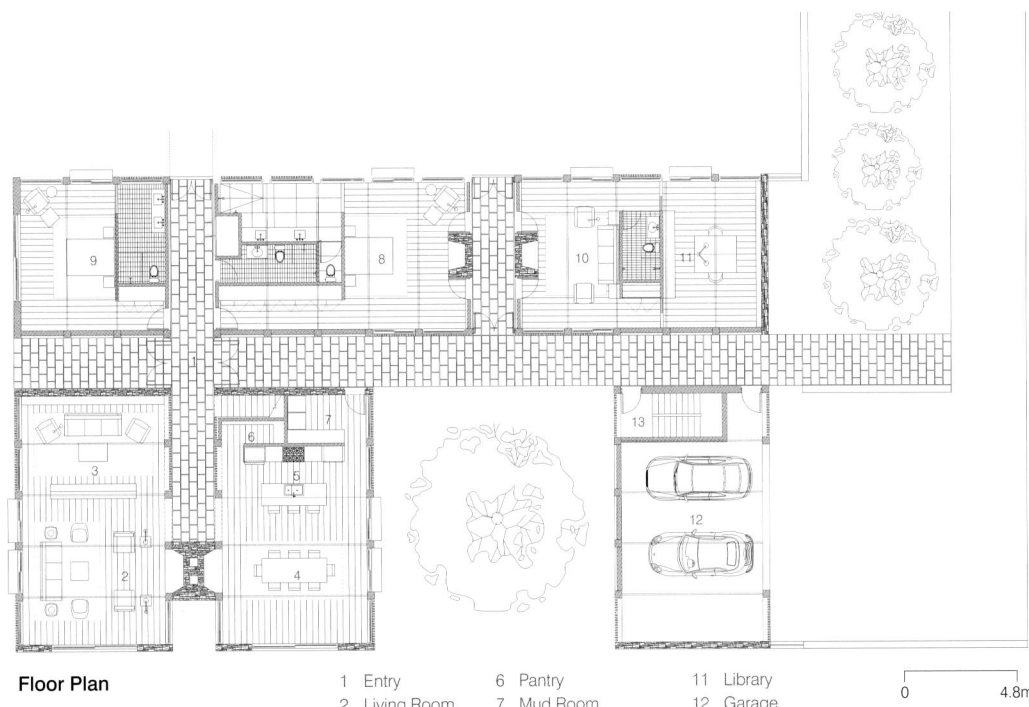

Floor Plan

1. Entry
2. Living Room
3. Media Room
4. Dining Room
5. Kitchen
6. Pantry
7. Mud Room
8. Master Suite
9. Guest Suite
10. Study / Guest Room
11. Library
12. Garage
13. Up to Loft

Red Hook Residence

Acknowledgements

We would like to thank the outstanding members of our staff, without whom the projects we have designed would not be what they are, especially our associates, Takaaki Kawabata, who has been with the firm since 1998; Matthew Jasion, since 2003; and Camaal Benoit, since 2006.

Our appreciation also goes to the individuals whose careful attention to detail contributed greatly to the creation of this monograph, in particular our special projects director, Heidi Engstrom, who led the effort; to Young Ha Mok, whose beautiful drawings predominately illustrate the projects, along with those of Chie Ikeda and Angie Winston; and to Nicolas Michael / ArX NY for their beautiful renderings. We also extend our gratitude to all of the talented photographers who have captured our designs over the past 20 years, especially Scott Frances, Mikiko Kikuyama, Eric Laignel, Paul Warchol, and Michael Weschler.

Thanks, too, to Susan Becher, for her tireless support; to Paul Latham, our intrepid publisher; to Andrew Sessa, for his thoughtful introduction, which captures our intentions with succinct clarity; and to Rod Gilbert, for his elegant book design.

Lastly, we would like to acknowledge our inspiring clients, many of whom have been on this journey with us for much of the past 20 years, and all of whom have shared our passion for design and the role that it plays in our lives.

Mark Janson
Hal Goldstein
Steven Scuro
Partners, Janson Goldstein LLP
New York, NY – September 2015

Photography Credits

Ben Rahn: 76–77, 79–85

Bill Waldorf: 136–139

Calvin Klein Inc.: 36–39

Dinex Group: 46–51

Eric Laignel: 74–75, 101–102

Grazia Casa: 193

Janson Goldstein LLP: 45, 256

Michael Desjardins: 74

Michael Weschler: 26–27, 29, 140–141, 143

Michelle Litvin: 106–111

Mikiko Kikuyama: 13–25, 31–35, 40–41, 62–73, 87–101, 103, 112–115, 128–129, 131–135, 158–163, 186–191, 212–219, 222–234, 236–247

Nikolas Koenig: 196–197

Paul Warchol: 55–57, 144–145, 165, 194–196

Rick Lew: 166–167

Rosky & Associates Inc.: 146–149

Scott Frances: 175–179, 201, 203–211

Toshi Yoshimi: 105

Every effort has been made to trace the original source of copyright material contained in this book. The publishers would be pleased to hear from copyright holders to rectify any errors or omissions.

The information and illustrations in this publication have been prepared and supplied by the architect. While all reasonable efforts have been made to ensure accuracy, the publishers do not, under any circumstances, accept responsibility for errors, omissions and representations express or implied.

Varick Street, 1995

Janson Goldstein LLP
Founded, 180 Varick Street, New York City, 1995
jansongoldstein.com